MAN UNITED
CHAMPIONS 2000

CARLING
CHAMPIONS

Shoot ANNUAL 2001
CONTENTS

All this PLUS great quizzes, action-packed
posters , your favourite Shoot features
and much, much more!

Published by

Pedigree®
Books Ltd

under license from

ipc
COUNTRY
&LEISURE
MEDIA

**Pedigree Books Ltd
The Old Rectory
Matford Lane
Exeter
Devon
EX2 4PS**

**All Editorial, Design and
Reprographics by Final
Score Ltd
finalscore@compuserve.com**

**Photography: Allsport and
Action Images with special
thanks to Eugene, Mark,
Mark and Richard**

Tm and © **IPC Media Ltd
2000**

ENGLAND 2000

Shoot

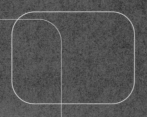

THE SUPER
STRIKERS

**YORKE
KANU
FLO
BRIDGES
SHEARER
PHILLIPS
WALLACE
VIDUKA
OWEN
CAMPBELL**

Also including...

Best of...In the House and Hanging Out

Shoot Interactive

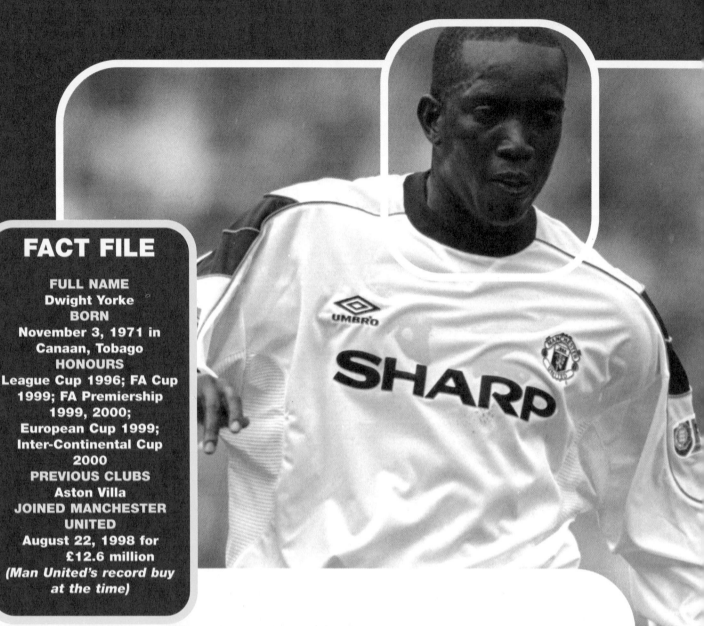

FACT FILE

FULL NAME
Dwight Yorke
BORN
November 3, 1971 in Canaan, Tobago
HONOURS
League Cup 1996; FA Cup 1999; FA Premiership 1999, 2000; European Cup 1999; Inter-Continental Cup 2000
PREVIOUS CLUBS
Aston Villa
JOINED MANCHESTER UNITED
August 22, 1998 for £12.6 million
(Man United's record buy at the time)

SUPER STRIKERS
DWIGHT YORKE
Man Utd & Trinidad

He always plays with a big grin on his face, but Dwight Yorke is one of the strikers that defenders fear most. The Manchester United ace has developed into one of Europe's best in his two seasons with the Red Devils and his brilliant skills and ace finishing make him a joy to watch - and give him plenty to smile about!

His Great Goals

Venue: Wembley
Match: Aston Villa 3 Leeds 0
Comp: League Cup Final
Date: March 24, 1996
There's only one team in it as Villa cruise through the Coca-Cola Cup Final at Wembley. Savo Milosevic puts Villa ahead, Ian Taylor makes it 2-0 and Dwight Yorke caps a brilliant display by scoring a last-gasp third to secure his first senior medal.

Venue: Old Trafford
Match: Man Utd 4 Charlton 1
Comp: FA Premiership
Date: September 9, 1998
Making his home debut for United, record signing Dwight Yorke has plenty to prove to the Old Trafford faithful. By the end of the match he has won them over. Two goals and a vibrant, hard-running performance give United's home supporters their first glimpse of a new hero.

Venue: Nou Camp, Barcelona
Match: Barcelona 3 Man Utd 3
Comp: Champions League
Date: November 25, 1999
Alongside his partner-in-goals, Andy Cole, Yorke gives another memorable display. The pair run rings around Barca's famous defence, with Yorke scoring twice and Cole once.

Venue: Old Trafford
Match: Man United 2 Inter Milan 0
Comp: Champions League QF first leg
Date: March 3, 1999
Two headed strikes from Yorkie help United to a crushing win over their Italian rivals. The first comes from a David Beckham cross early on, the second just before half-time leaves United in dreamland as the Old Trafford club take a giant stride towards a Semi-Final place in the Champions League.

DID YOU KNOW?
Dwight nearly didn't make it as a pro footballer - coz he got knocked down by a car when he was a kid. Luckily for Dwight, a doctor was passing by and rushed the youngster straight off to hospital. He's left a few 'keepers feeling pretty sick since then!

MAN UTD ODD SPOT
A St Bernard dog that was helping United collect money at a fair turned up lost on the doorstep of a wealthy brewer called John Davies. He traced the dog's owner, Reds captain Harry Stafford, and was so moved by the club's financial troubles that he paid off their debts, became chairman and helped them move to Old Trafford!

DID YOU KNOW?
Yorkie is best mates with the West Indies cricketer Brian Lara. The pair grew up together in Trinidad and had trials for the island's Under-12s football team. He's a decent batsman himself and also plays golf to a good standard.

HOW HE RATES

Speed		4
Strength		4
Shooting		4
Finishing		4
Dribbling		3
Heading		4

SUPER STRIKERS
NWANKWO KANU
Arsenal & Nigeria

This tall and gangly striker has got more tricks up his sleeve than a top magician. Superb skill and great strength in the air make him a big handful for defenders, and he's always likely to try the unexpected... often with spectacular results!

FACT FILE

FULL NAME
Nwankwo Kanu
BORN
August 1, 1975 in Owerri
HONOURS
Dutch League 1994, 1995, 1996; Dutch Super Cup 1994, 1995; European Cup 1995; World Club Cup 1995; Olympic Gold medal 1996
PREVIOUS CLUBS
Federation Works Iwanyanwu (both Nigeria), Ajax, Inter Milan
JOINED ARSENAL
Feb 4, 1999 for £4.5 million

HOW HE RATES

Speed		3
Strength		4
Shooting		4
Finishing		3
Dribbling		4
Heading		4

DID YOU KNOW?

The brilliant striker with the size 14 feet is one of the most exciting performers in the Premiership. But when he was with Inter Milan in Italy he underwent major heart surgery which seriously threatened his future in the game.

ARSENAL ODD SPOT

The Gunners reckon that a dead horse brings them luck! The spooky pony - no relation to Tony Adams we're told - died in a construction accident during the building of Highbury and lies buried beneath what is now the ground's famous North Bank.

Dreamcast

His Great Goals

Venue: The Riverside Stadium
Match: Middlesbrough 1 Arsenal 6
Comp: FA Premiership
Date: April 24, 1999
Arsenal steamroller their Premiership opponents, with Kanu grabbing an outrageous goal to cap a fine performance. He has already scored once when Lee Dixon swings in a low cross after 60 minutes. The defence can only stand and watch as Kanu leaps into the air and flicks the ball in with his right heel - which is round the back of his left leg. It's a moment of absolute brilliance and even the Boro fans applaud his skill.

Venue: White Hart Lane
Match: Tottenham 1 Arsenal 3
Comp: FA Premiership
Date: May 5, 1999
Kanu settles the North London derby with a great piece of individual skill. With Arsenal already 2-1 up, a pass comes to Kanu's feet five minutes from time. With a deft flick he lifts the ball over defender Luke Young before spinning past his hapless marker to smash the ball past Ian Walker in the Spurs goal.

Venue: Stamford Bridge
Match: Chelsea 2 Arsenal 3
Comp: FA Premiership
Date: October 23, 1999
A magnificent hat-trick for the Nigerian master - and his third goal is the pick of the lot. With 90 minutes on the clock, Kanu slips past Ed de Goey on the byeline way out to the left of the goal. He glances up and then bends his shot over the heads of Marcel Desailly and Frank Leboeuf on the Chelsea line and into the net. It is one of the greatest Premiership goals of all time and wins the game for The Gunners.

DID YOU KNOW?
Kanu's family have not been allowed by the government to move to England from Nigeria. As a result, the player says he is very lonely and often goes out in London just to find people to talk to! He has also said that he may leave Arsenal if things don't get better.

Shoot 11

TORE ANDRE FLO
Chelsea & Norway

He doesn't look much like a world class footballer, but the lanky Norwegian has proved to be among the planet's best when it comes to sticking the ball in the net. Strong in the air, but equally skilful on the ground, this £300,000 bargain is a nightmare for opposition defenders at home and abroad.

FACT FILE

FULL NAME
Tore Andre Flo
BORN
June 15, 1973 in Strin, Norway
HONOURS
League Cup 1998; European Cup-Winners' Cup 1998, European Super Cup 1998; FA Cup 2000
PREVIOUS CLUBS
Tromso, Sogndal, Brann Bergen (all Norway)
JOINED CHELSEA
August 4, 1997 for £300,000

DID YOU KNOW?

Back home in Norway, Tore Andre is nicknamed 'Flonaldo' after he scored twice for his country in a 4-2 win against Brazil in a friendly in 1997!

DID YOU KNOW?

Tore comes from a successful footballing family. His older brother, Havard, is also a Norwegian international and plays his club football for Wolves. Cousin Jostein, another international in the family, used to play for Sheffield United.

CHELSEA ODD SPOT

If you want to get ahead, get a dog. That seems to be the way to set up a successful football club. In much the same way as Man United's present success can be traced back to the actions of a pesky pooch, so can Chelsea's. Way back in 1904 the Mears brothers purchased Stamford Bridge and were quickly made a tempting offer by the Great Western Railway, who wanted to use the site as a coal dump. The idea of a quick profit appealed to Gus Mears, but his friend Frederick Parker tried to persuade the developer that the ground was perfect for football. During their meeting, Mears' dog bit Parker on the leg, and Mears was so impressed with the cool manner in which Parker reacted that he decided to take his friend's advice - and founded Chelsea Football Club!

His Great Goals

Venue: Stade Velodrome, Marseille
Match: Brazil 1 Norway 2
Comp: World Cup finals
Date: June 23, 1998
Flo scores his third goal in two games against Brazil - but this is by far the most important. With seven minutes of their World Cup group game against Brazil remaining, Norway are a goal down and look to be on their way out of the tournament. But a superb pass from Stig-Inge Bjornebye finds Flo on the edge of the Brazil area and the striker shakes off Junior Baiano to score with a brilliant cross-shot and set in motion Norway's great recovery.

Venue: Stamford Bridge
Match: Chelsea 2 Tottenham 0
Comp: FA Premiership
Date: December 19, 1998
Chelsea are already a goal to the good when Blues' Dan Petrescu

manages to get free down the right flank and send over a perfect cross which Flo rockets into the net with a flying header. His goal helps take Chelsea to the top of the Premiership.

Venue: Stamford Bridge
Match: Chelsea 3 Barcelona 1
Comp: Champions League
Date: April 5, 2000
On an extraordinary night at Stamford Bridge, Tore Andre strikes twice to tame mighty Barcelona. Chelsea give a perfect display of counter-attacking football, with Flo taking full advantage to tuck away two memorable goals, the second a brilliant finish after being put through on goal. Flo also scores in the second leg in Spain but Chelsea still crash out of the Cup.

HOW HE RATES

Speed	3
Strength	4
Shooting	4
Finishing	4
Dribbling	4
Heading	5

Shoot 13

MICHAEL BRIDGES
Leeds United

Signed from Sunderland for a then club record £5 million, Michael Bridges started the 1999-2000 campaign as an unknown striker at Elland Road - and finished it as Leeds' leading scorer. Alongside other youngsters like Alan Smith, Jonathan Woodgate and Harry Kewell, England Under-21 international Michael has taken the Premiership by storm.

FACT FILE

FULL NAME
Michael Bridges
BORN
August 5, 1978 in
North Shields
HONOURS
First Division title
1996, 1999
PREVIOUS CLUBS
Sunderland
JOINED LEEDS
July 1999 for £5 million

DID YOU KNOW?

Despite being a Sunderland fan, Michael's all-time hero is ex-Newcastle winger Chris Waddle. "He was my hero, the player I admired the most," admits Michael. "I managed to play alongside him for a while when I was at Sunderland, it was amazing."

LEEDS ODD SPOT

Leeds United were formed in 1919 by a group of local businessmen led by solicitor Alf Masser, after the original Leeds City club were disbanded by the Football Association after allegations of illegal payments to players. Naughty, naughty!

DID YOU KNOW?

In 1999-2000 Michael narrowly missed out on becoming the first Leeds player for nearly 10 years to notch 20 League goals in a season. Michael finished the campaign on 19, just two behind the total managed by Lee Chapman in the 1990-91 campaign.

His Great Goals

Venue: Bramall Lane
Match: Sheff Utd 0 Sunderland 4
Comp: Nationwide First Division
Date: November 28, 1998
Bridges scores twice to take his tally to ten in 12 games as Sunderland cement their place at the top of the First Division. Bridges' performance leaves his experienced strike partner, Niall Quinn, purring: "Michael is a terrific footballer. A natural."

Venue: The Dell
Match: Southampton 0 Leeds 3
Comp: FA Premiership
Date: August 11, 1999
Bridges announces his arrival at Leeds with a superbly taken hat-trick on his debut for the club. He opens his account with a long range chip over 'keeper Paul Jones, follows up with a tap-in from a Danny Mills cross and then completes his treble by heading home from an Ian Harte corner.

Venue: Goodison Park
Match: Everton 4 Leeds 4
Comp: FA Premiership
Date: October 23, 1999
Bridges is outstanding as Leeds come from behind three times to earn a draw at Everton. He scores twice, with the second a strike straight out of the top drawer. Bridges plays a one-two with Darren Huckerby on 67 minutes before flicking the ball up and lifting it over 'keeper Paul Gerrard.

Venue: Lokomotiv Stadium
Match: Lok. Moscow 0 Leeds 3
Comp: UEFA Cup
Date: November 4, 1999
Vibrant Leeds put on a great display to dump the Russian giants out of the tournament. Bridges scores twice to cap a quality all-round performance, with both goals showing the striker's close range poaching skills as Leeds march on in Europe.

HOW HE RATES

Speed	4
Strength	3
Shooting	4
Finishing	3
Dribbling	3
Heading	3

SUPER STRIKERS
ALAN SHEARER
Newcastle & England

An inspirational figure for club and country for the last eight years, Alan Shearer retired from international football after Euro 2000. He has topped 30 Premiership goals in three of the last seven seasons and is regarded as one of the best strikers in the world. Now playing for Newcastle, the club he supported as a boy.

FACT FILE

FULL NAME
Alan Shearer
BORN
August 13, 1970
in Newcastle
HONOURS
FA Premiership 1995; PFA Player of the Year 1995, 1997; Football Writers' Footballer of the Year 1994
PREVIOUS CLUBS
Southampton, Blackburn
JOINED NEWCASTLE
July 30, 1996 for £15 million (a British record at the time)

NEWCASTLE ODD SPOT

At Christmas in 1996, Newcastle were 12 points clear of second placed Man United and seemed to be cruising to a first League title since 1927. But Kevin Keegan's side lost their nerve and blew the title, losing out to the eventual double-winners from Old Trafford.

DID YOU KNOW?

Shearer is the Premiership's all-time leading scorer, with a total of 176 goals to his credit. In 1995-96 he became the first player since the Second World War to score more than 30 top division goals in a season in three successive campaigns

DID YOU KNOW?

Alan won the Golden Boot after top scoring at Euro 96. His total of five goals was two more than any other player. What made his record even more amazing was that prior to the tournament he had failed to find the net in 12 internationals for England.

His Great Goals

Venue: The Dell
Match: Southampton 4 Arsenal 2
Comp: First Division
Date: April 9, 1988
At just 17 years, 140 days old, Alan becomes the youngest player to score a hat-trick on his full debut as he lashes three goals past Arsenal 'keeper John Lukic.

Venue: Wembley
Match: England 2 France 0
Comp: Friendly international
Date: February 19, 1992
Another debut, another goal. Having been called up by Graham Taylor, Shearer proves his good form at club level is no flash in the pan.

Venue: Anfield
Match: Liverpool 2 Blackburn 1
Comp: FA Premiership
Date: May 14, 1995
Shearer nets his 37th and final goal of the 1994-95 campaign as unfashionable Blackburn win the Premiership title.

Venue: Wembley
Match: England 1 Switzerland 1
Comp: Euro 96 Group game
Date: June 8, 1996
Shearer ends his two-year goal drought for England with a 20-yard screamer into the top corner.

Venue: Wembley
Match: England 4 Holland 1
Comp: Euro 96 Group game
Date: June 18, 1996
Super Al lashes in a right foot thunderbolt to make it 3-0 as England take the Dutch apart.

HOW HE RATES

Speed		3
Strength		5
Shooting		4
Finishing		4
Dribbling		3
Heading		5

SUPER STRIKERS
KEVIN PHILLIPS
SUNDERLAND & ENGLAND

FACT FILE

FULL NAME
Kevin Phillips
BORN
July 25, 1973
in Hitchin
HONOURS
First Division title 1999
PREVIOUS CLUBS
Watford
JOINED SUNDERLAND
July 17, 1997 for
£325,000

DID YOU KNOW?

As a trainee at Southampton, Kevin cleaned the boots of Alan Shearer - who he would later partner up front for England. But Saints dumped him becausemanager Chris Nicholl felt the youngster would never make it as a professional footballer. Maybe that's not surprising - Kevin played at right-back in those days!

DID YOU KNOW?

On April 28, 1999 Phillips made his debut for England in an international friendly against Hungary in Budapest. It signalled aremarkable turnaround in fortunes for the young striker, who just four and-a-half years earlier had been working in a warehouse stacking shelves while playing part-time with non-League Baldock Town.

HOW HE RATES

Speed	4
Strength	4
Shooting	4
Finishing	5
Dribbling	3
Heading	4

SUNDERLAND ODD SPOT

After moving from Roker Park to the Stadium of Light in 1997, the club decided to drop their old nickname, The Rokerites. A fans' poll was held and The Black Cats came top. Two black lions are on the club badge.

The scoring star of last season, Kevin Phillips rocked the Premiership by rattling in a whopping 30 goals en route to becoming the League's top striker. Quick, strong and with lightning reactions around the box, Phillips played a huge role in Sunderland's impressive first season back in the top flight. It was form that won him a place in England's Euro 2000 squad.

His Great Goals

Venue: Stadium of Light
Match: Sunderland 3 Man City 1
Comp: First Division
Date: August 15, 1997
A bargain buy from Watford, £325,000 signing Kevin Phillips makes his Sunderland debut, and has the fans on his side from the opening minutes. He announces his intentions by rattling in a goal after 84 minutes to celebrate his arrival in style.

Venue: Gigg Lane
Match: Bury 2 Sunderland 5
Comp: First Division
Date: April 13, 1999
Phillips puts four past Bury 'keeper Dean Kiely to help Sunderland confirm promotion to the Premiership.

Venue: St. James' Park
Match: Newcastle 1 Sunderland 2
Comp: FA Premiership
Date: August 25, 1999
The critics said that Phillips would never make it in the Premiership, but the striker had already started to prove them wrong before this game. In the white-hot atmosphere of the north east derby he pounces to score again as Sunderland win 2-1.

Venue: Pride Park
Match: Derby 0 Sunderland 5
Comp: FA Premiership
Date: September 18, 1999
A brilliant and brutally taken hat-trick confirms Phillips' arrival on the big stage as Derby are torn apart. He rocks The Rams with strikes in the 41st, 52nd and 84th minutes, to leave rival boss Jim Smith purring: "He's good enough for England, that's for sure."

Venue: Stadium of Light
Match: Sunderland 4 Chelsea 1
Comp: FA Premiership
Date: December 4, 1999
Super Kev scores one of the goals of the season as Championship hopefuls Chelsea are handed a footballing lesson. He crashes in an unstoppable 25-yard half-volley to light up the Stadium of Light.

ROD WALLACE
Rangers

A Championship winner in England and Scotland, hot Rod has been a nightmare for defenders for many years. Despite being only 5ft 7ins tall, he scores a fair few goals with his head and his lightning pace makes him one of the sharpest strikers around the penalty area.

FACT FILE

FULL NAME
Rodney Wallace
BORN
October 2, 1969 in Lewisham, London
HONOURS
First Division Championship 1992; Scottish League title 1999, 2000; SFA Cup 1999, 2000; Scottish League Cup 1999
PREVIOUS CLUBS
Southampton, Leeds
JOINED RANGERS
July 17, 1998 on a free transfer from Leeds

DID YOU KNOW?

Rod is one of three Wallace brothers who have played League football. They all started their careers at Southampton, with eldest brother Danny going on to play for Manchester United and England. Rod and his twin brother Ray were at Leeds together.

DID YOU KNOW?

Rod has represented England at Under-21 and B level but has never followed his brother Danny in to the senior side. He was involved in England training camps but failed to make the breakthrough despite finishing top scorer at each of his three clubs.

HOW HE RATES

Speed	4
Strength	3
Shooting	4
Finishing	4
Dribbling	4
Heading	3

His Great Goals

Venue: Ewood Park
Match: Blackburn 3 Leeds 4
Comp: FA Premiership
Date: September 14, 1997
A thrilling, see-saw game ends up in Leeds' favour after Wallace steps in with two crucial goals. The second of them, a glorious curling finish, is a candidate for goal of the season.

Venue: Tynecastle
Match: Hearts 2 Rangers 1
Comp: Scottish Premier League
Date: August 2, 1998
Expecting to be overshadowed by big money signings such as Stephane Guivarc'h and Andrei Kanchelskis, Rod Wallace gets his Rangers career off to a flyer with a goal just 28 minutes into his debut. It's not enough to stop 'Gers losing to their Edinburgh rivals, though.

Venue: Hampden Park
Match: Celtic 0 Rangers 1
Comp: Scottish Cup Final
Date: May 29, 1999
The former Southampton and Leeds striker is the star of the show as Rangers round off their fantastic season with a Cup Final win over old rivals Celtic. Wallace snatches the game's only goal after 48 minutes with a close range strike to complete a trophy treble for his side.

Venue: Ibrox
Match: Rangers 6 Motherwell 2
Comp: Scottish Premier League
Date: March 18, 2000
Rangers' march towards a world record 49th League title continues as Motherwell are thrashed at Ibrox. Wallace lashes in his second hat-trick in three weeks - after 20, 42 and 70 minutes - to send his side 12 points clear at the top of the League table.

RANGERS ODD SPOT
Question of Sport team captain and TV pundit Ally McCoist is the most successful Rangers striker of all time. The former Scotland international scored a massive 355 goals for the club during his 13 year career at Ibrox between 1985 and 1998.

SUPER STRIKERS
MARK VIDUKA
Celtic & Australia

When Celtic lost Henrik Larsson through injury last season, many thought they would struggle to score goals. But they reckoned without the class of Mark Viduka who ended the campaign as Scotland's leading scorer, with 25 Premier League goals to his name.

DID YOU KNOW?
Nicknamed the 'V-Bomber' by Aussie fans, he has not always had such a good relationship with the supporters. While at Croatia Zagreb he found it difficult to return home for games and some fans were so upset that he even received death threats!

DID YOU KNOW?
Mark had a stormy start to his Celtic career. Having signed from Croatia Zagreb for £3 million, the player disappeared just days later. He returned to Australia saying he had depression, and that he was not mentally prepared to play football.

FACT FILE

FULL NAME
Marko Viduka
BORN
October 9, 1975
in Australia
HONOURS
Scottish PFA Player of the
Year 1999-2000
PREVIOUS CLUBS
Melbourne Knights,
Croatia Zagreb
JOINED CELTIC
November 20, 1998 for
£3 million

CELTIC ODD SPOT

Celtic just loved playing Aberdeen
last term. The two clubs met five
times in the 1999-2000 season and in
those matches, The Bhoys clocked
up 23 goals with The Dons scoring
just once in reply!

HOW HE RATES

Speed	▬▬▬▬	4
Strength	▬▬▬▬	4
Shooting	▬▬▬▬	4
Finishing	▬▬▬▬	4
Dribbling	▬▬▬	3
Heading	▬▬▬▬	4

His Great Goals

Venue: Pittodrie
Match: Aberdeen 1 Celtic 5
Comp: Scottish Premier Division
Date: March 14, 1999
In his first start for Celtic after his on-off
transfer, Viduka shows just why The Bhoys
were so keen to bring him to Glasgow. The
big Australian scores twice - after 27 and 47
minutes - as Aberdeen are battered.

Venue: Celtic Park
Match: Celtic 2 Dundee Utd 0
Comp: Scottish Cup Semi-Final
Date: April 10, 1999
Viduka strikes past goalkeeper Sieb Dykstra
after 39 minutes to clinch a place at
Hampden Park and a Scottish Cup Final date
with bitter rivals Rangers.

Venue: Pittodrie
Match: Aberdeen 0 Celtic 5
Comp: Scottish Premier League
Date: August 1, 1999
The Dons are in the firing line once more, as
Viduka kicks-off the 1999-2000 campaign in
style. He scores twice - once with a header
from a Lubomir Moravcik cross, the other a
close range tap-in.

Venue: Celtic Park
Match: Celtic 7 Aberdeen 0
Comp: Scottish Premier League
Date: October 16, 1999
Poor old Aberdeen! Aussie hit-man Viduka
goes one better as he notches his
first hat-trick in Scotland to see off the
struggling east coast side once again.

Venue: Celtic Park
Match: Celtic 5 Kilmarnock 1
Comp: Scottish Premier League
Date: October 30, 1999
Another day, another hat-trick. Viduka's
triple comes in the space of five
remarkable minutes. The opener is the
result of an intelligent through ball
from Ian Wright, which Viduka steers past
Killie 'keeper Michael Watt. It is
followed by two near identical far post
headers to seal another fine victory for the
Bhoys and cement the Australian star's
status as a striker to be feared.

FACT FILE
FULL NAME
Michael James Owen
BORN
December 14, 1979
in Chester
PREVIOUS CLUBS
None
HONOURS
PFA Young Player of
the Year 1998
JOINED LIVERPOOL
December 18, 1996
from trainee

SUPER STRIKERS
MICHAEL OWEN
Liverpool & England

The lightning fast Owen is one of the world's most dangerous strikers. He burst onto the England scene at World Cup 1998 and has been setting scoring records throughout his short career. Still only 20, he is set to be a star for the next 10 years.

His Great Goals

Venue: Selhurst Park
Match: Wimbledon 2 Liverpool 1
Comp: FA Premiership
Date: May 6, 1997
Teenager Michael Owen starts as he means to go on. Having come on for his first Liverpool game, as a substitute for Patrik Berger, Owen steals in to nick a consolation goal for the Reds.

Venue: Hillsborough
Match: Sheff Wed 3 Liverpool 3
Comp: FA Premiership
Date: February 14, 1998
The pundits are purring as Owen tears Wednesday apart. "I knew he was good, but hell, not that good," admits Owls boss Ron Atkinson after the game.

Venue: Mohammed V Stadium, Morocco
Match: Morocco 0 England 1
Comp: International friendly
Date: May 27, 1998
Owen opens his international goal account in his fourth appearance for England. Steve McManaman hits the ball over the top and Owen spins past his marker before sliding the ball past goalkeeper Benzakri.

Venue: Saint Etienne, France
Match: England 2 Argentina 2
Comp: World Cup Second Round
Date: June 30, 1998
Michael who? That was the question the world's press were asking before this crucial World Cup match. Sixteen minutes after kick-off they had their answer. Picking up a pass from David Beckham on the halfway line, Owen turns and heads straight for goal, his pace leaves defenders in his wake before he sidesteps Roberto Ayala and sends a rocket shot past 'keeper Carlos Roa.

LIVERPOOL ODD SPOT

If it hadn't been for Everton, Liverpool might never have existed! Having won their first League title in 1891 - whilst playing at Anfield - Everton had a major bust-up with landlord John Houlding over an increase in rent and walked out. Houlding started a new club and even tried to call them Everton! The FA wouldn't allow that, so he reluctantly changed the name to Liverpool.

DID YOU KNOW?

As a kid Michael was a mad keen Everton supporter and Gary Lineker was his hero! He played for the Toffees' youth teams on several occasions as well. His dad, Terry, played for Everton in the 1960s as well as a number of other League clubs.

DID YOU KNOW?

Michael reckons he will never top the goal he netted for England Schoolboys against Scotland. He picked up the ball from the kick-off and dribbled to the edge of the Scottish box before hitting the ball into the top corner!

HOW HE RATES

Speed	5
Strength	4
Shooting	4
Finishing	4
Dribbling	4
Heading	3

SUPER STRIKERS
KEVIN
CAMPBELL
Everton

Kevin Campbell made his name as a young hit-man with Arsenal in the early 1990s. After a few seasons out of the limelight he has shot back to prominence over the last couple of years with Everton. Big, strong and quick he is a handful for any defence and is considered the number one striker at Goodison Park.

FACT FILE

FULL NAME
Kevin Joseph Campbell
BORN
February 4, 1970 in Lambeth, London
HONOURS
League Cup 1993, FA Cup 1993; European Cup-Winners' Cup 1994; First Division title 1998
PREVIOUS CLUBS
Arsenal, Leyton Orient (loan), Leicester City (loan), Nottingham Forest, Trabzonspor (Turkey)
JOINED EVERTON
May 1999 for £3 million after initially joining Everton on loan two months earlier

DID YOU KNOW?

Kevin Campbell moved to Everton after being racially abused by the chairman of his previous club, Trabzonspor in Turkey. Mehmet Ali Yilmaz made rude remarks about Kevin on a TV show, and the player was so disgusted he walked out on the club.

DID YOU KNOW?

Campbell scored five League goals in 17 games for Trabzonspor, but the player is the first to admit that things were a little, well, different over there. "They once brought a dead sheep out onto the pitch before a game," he recalls. "They got the players to stick their fingers into the blood and put it on our faces. You didn't have to do it - but if you did the fans went crazy!" We take it they don't do that at Goodison Park then, Kev?"

His Great Goals

Venue: Highbury
Match: Arsenal 1 Paris St. Germain 0
Comp: European Cup-Winners' Cup Semi-Final
Date: April 12, 1994
Campbell strikes after just six minutes to clinch the second-leg of this tie after the first match in Paris had finished all square. His goal, against a PSG side inspired by David Ginola, takes Arsenal to their first European Final for 14 years.

Venue: Highfield Road
Match: Coventry 0 Nottingham Forest 3
Comp: FA Premiership
Date: August 17, 1996
Kevin Campbell gets the 1996-97 campaign off to a flying start by plundering a hat-trick in the opening game. His third goal is the best of the lot, as he picks up a weak clearance from Paul Williams and surges forward into the penalty area before unleashing a vicious shot past Steve Ogrizovic.

Venue: Goodison Park
Match: Everton 6 West Ham 0
Comp: FA Premiership
Date: May 8, 1999
The powerful striker picks up the Premiership 'Player of the Month' award for April prior to the match - and celebrates by scoring a hat-trick to ensure Everton's survival in the top flight. Pick of the bunch is his second - a delicate chip over the head of Shaka Hislop.

Venue: Anfield
Match: Liverpool 0 Everton 1
Comp: FA Premiership
Date: September 28, 1999
The Mersey derby is settled after a crisp series of passes between Nick Barmby and Francis Jeffers sets Campbell free, and the striker cracks in a blistering winner.

EVERTON ODD SPOT

Everton's nickname, The Toffees, comes from 'Ye Ancient Everton Toffee House', which was right next to the pub where the club was formed. They were originally known as the Black Watch after their distinctive playing strip of black shirt with a red sash.

HOW HE RATES

Speed		4
Strength		5
Shooting		4
Finishing		3
Dribbling		3
Heading		4

THE BEST OF
IN THE HOUSE WITH...

DANNY MURPHY "I'm pretty domesticated. The only thing I can't do is the ironing. These two shirts are special to me. The Liverpool one I wore for my first game against Manchester United, while the other shirt is from when I scored a hat-trick for the England youth side."

EIDUR GUDJOHNSEN "This giant photograph of the Reebok Stadium is in the main reception. It says 'Anything's Possible'."

ANDY MYERS AND MICHAEL DUBERRY "Doobs is round here every day - and every day he'll do his best to get on my nerves! No, seriously, he's good to have around and it helps to have somebody to bounce conversation off. He chills out here and we go out on the town together."

JOHN CURTIS "I never get enough time to go fishing because of training. My other half, Gemma, will tell you otherwise, but I'd certainly like to get down to the river more often. I once put some maggots in a box and left them in the fridge, Gemma went mad. My best catch was a 7lbs barbel."

STEVE FINNAN "Here's our trophy cabinet, and one of my favourite trophies is the AXA Giantkillers Trophy we won after Fulham's FA Cup win over Aston Villa a couple of seasons ago. The glass trophy cabinet was a gift from all the lads to the chairman for all the good work he's done."

ADE AKINBIYI "Here's the head of our chairman, Sir Jack Hayward - but he's a bit better looking in the flesh! He's the main man here and is so passionate about the club. He's ploughed loads of money into Wolves."

DEAN KIELY "I used to spend summers helping out my dad and brother-in-law with their building business. It came in handy when I built a new front wall. I quite enjoy mucking in and getting my hands dirty, but I'd rather keep goal, especially for my club Charlton in the Premiership."

NICKY WEAVER "Meet the missus! You might wonder why on earth Lara Croft is a permanent fixture at Maine Road, but it's all to do with Eidos, who are the club sponsors. It's quite handy having them on board, though, because we get sorted out with all our PlayStation games."

Shoot INTERACTIVE

WHO ARE YA?

READ THE CLUES AND SEE IF YOU CAN SUSS OUT THE IDENTITY OF THE MYSTERY PLAYERS...

I play for a team in the north
I've won caps for England
My debut was against Luxembourg last season
I used to play at Portman Road
I'm not like my surname says

_ _ _ R _ _ D _ _ _ _

DO YOU KNOW YOUR SUPER STRIKERS

HAVE YOU BEEN PAYING ATTENTION? IF YOU HAVE, THEN YOU'LL HAVE NO PROBLEMS ANSWERING THESE TERRIFIC TEASERS...

1 For which country does Nwankwo Kanu play international football?

2 Chelsea paid just £300,000 for Norwegian hit-man Tore Andre Flo. True or false?

3 Who was Michael Bridges' all-time hero?

4 In what position did Kevin Phillips play during his Southampton days? Was it defence, midfield or up front?

5 Who did Mark Viduka play for before he joined Celtic?

6 What was special about Kevin Campbell's goal against Paris St. Germain in April 1994?

I come from abroad
I score spectacular goals
I have advertised shampoo on television
I've won a Cup at Wembley
Many of my fans are girls

D _ _ _ _ I _ _ _ _

WORDSEARCH

Hidden in the giant wordsearch below are the names of 20 of the British game's top strikers. You'll find them vertically, horizontally, diagonally or even backwards. To give you a helping hand, we've found the first one for you...but can you spot the rest?

THE STARS YOU'RE LOOKING FOR ARE:
Michael BRIDGES, Kevin CAMPBELL, Andy COLE, Tony COTTEE, Tore Andre FLO,
Robbie FOWLER, Shaun GOATER, Emile HESKEY, David JOHNSON, Nwankwo KANU,
Clive MENDONCA, Michael OWEN, Kevin PHILLIPS, Sergei REBROV, Hamilton RICARD,
Alan SHEARER, Mark VIDUKA, Rod WALLACE, Dean WINDASS, Dwight YORKE

K	A	N	U	F	T	E	F	O	W	L	E	R	R
A	C	E	L	X	Q	S	L	R	A	R	R	E	I
A	N	G	K	S	A	C	O	T	T	E	E	B	C
R	O	E	O	A	H	V	V	E	W	Q	C	R	A
Q	D	W	O	A	U	E	S	S	O	R	W	O	R
W	N	E	E	E	T	U	A	K	U	D	I	V	D
W	E	A	L	N	U	E	O	R	L	S	T	T	W
W	M	Q	L	T	T	U	R	W	E	M	M	O	Q
E	H	L	I	T	S	E	G	D	I	R	B	Q	L
J	O	H	N	S	O	N	I	N	T	W	L	I	C
W	S	W	E	K	K	T	N	O	W	I	W	M	A
F	I	M	A	A	E	E	T	T	I	S	J	E	M
A	P	H	I	L	L	I	P	S	N	V	A	E	P
A	W	R	C	O	L	E	I	U	D	K	L	K	B
B	S	O	O	T	U	A	M	R	A	W	J	R	E
A	S	S	E	B	C	W	C	U	S	E	R	O	L
E	L	L	N	I	W	F	H	E	S	K	E	Y	L

Quiz Answers on page 110-111

Shoot

STARS OF THE
FUTURE

**KEANE
COLE
DYER
GERRARD
BARRY**

Despite his name, and the fact that they were both born in Ireland, Robbie is not related to Man Utd's Roy Keane. As a free-scoring youngster he was watched by a number of scouts from England's top clubs, including Liverpool and Man Utd, but it was Wolves who snatched the player and signed him as a youth trainee in 1996.

His opening season in the English game was quite an eventful one, as Robbie played several games in the Wolves reserve side and was also picked for the Republic of Ireland's youth team. He made such an impact that on July 26, 1997, he was offered and signed a full pro contract with Wolves.

When the new season dawned on August 9, 1997, Robbie was handed a senior debut away to Norwich. It wasn't a bad start, either, as he scored both Wolves' goals in a 2-0 win! It was the first time in 37 years that a player had scored twice on his debut for the Molineux outfit. By the end of the season he had established himself as Wolves' top scorer.

Robbie was given a run-out in a 'B' international for Ireland, but the big one came on March 25, 1998, when he won his first senior cap as a sub in the 2-1 defeat by the Czech Republic in Oloumoc. He became Eire's second youngest ever international.

The youngster was thrilled a month later when he was picked to play against Argentina in his home town of Dublin. He had a good game, despite Ireland losing 2-0.

There was more good news to come in the summer of 1998, when he helped Ireland to a brilliant success in the European Youth Championship in Cyprus.

The following season had both good and bad times. Robbie continued to impress for both his club and his country and once again finished as top scorer for Wolves. But he also had two spells of injury and illness which put a blot on his season.

The 1999/2000 season started with another sensation, as Robbie switched to the Premiership with Coventry City in a whopping £6m deal. He made an immediate impact with Gordon Strachan's side, finishing the campaign as their top scorer with 12 goals in the League. At the end of the season he could look back with satisfaction, with perhaps the biggest compliment coming from Italy's Inter Milan who put in a £10m bid for his services!

STARS OF THE FUTURE

ROBBIE KEANE

NAME: Robert David Keane
BORN: Dublin on July 8, 1980
HONOURS: None
INTERNATIONAL: Republic of Ireland Youth, 'B', Full caps
SQUAD NUMBER: 7
MOST LIKELY TO BE: Banging in the goals. People said he wouldn't do it in the top flight, but Robbie proved the critics wrong with 12 League goals after his £6m transfer from Wolves to Coventry.

AChelsea supporter as a boy, Joe Cole was winning rave reviews even while still at school. He made his England schools debut against Wales on February 13, 1997, as England won 3-2 in what was a memorable debut for him.

His fame spread fast, and Joe trained with most of London's major clubs. There was a big temptation to join Chelsea, who were among the many clubs - including Man Utd - who expressed an interest. But in the end he chose West Ham "because they were the friendliest".

The youngster quickly advanced to the England youth side and then, even before he had made his senior debut for West Ham, Joe was called up to train with the full England squad. That was in November 1998.

On January 2, 1999, he made his eagerly-awaited first-team debut, coming on as substitute for Eyal Berkovic in the FA Cup Third Round 1-1 draw with Swansea.

A huge test was to follow eight days later, when he was on the bench at Old Trafford and then replaced Trevor Sinclair as West Ham lost 4-1 to Man Utd. The football world began to sit up and take notice. By the end of January 1999 he had made his first Premiership start, and was named man of the match, in a 0-0 draw against Wimbledon.

Despite all the glory, Joe had not turned his back on his youth team mates and in May 1999 he played in both legs of West Ham's FA Youth Cup Final against Coventry, which the Hammers won by an amazing 9-0.

Although he had scored freely throughout his early years, Joe was taking his time before finding the net for West Ham seniors. He finally cracked it in a Worthington Cup tie at Birmingham last season and couldn't stop grinning. A player's first goal is always one to remember!

February 22, 2000, was another big day for Joe, when he made his England U21 debut in a 1-0 win over Argentina. It was thought that he might jump straight from youth to senior international football, but Joe was keen to play for the U21s and Kevin Keegan agreed. Speculation was rife that Joe would be included in England's senior squad for Euro 2000, but a broken leg ruled him out of contention.

JOE COLE

NAME: Joseph John Cole
BORN: London on Nov 8, 1981
HONOURS: FA Youth Cup 1998
INTERNATIONAL: England Youth, U21 caps
SQUAD NUMBER: 26
MOST LIKELY TO BE: England's first 'world footballer of the year'. A gifted midfielder who works hard and has a huge box of tricks. He seems certain to become his country's playmaker and make a huge impact on the global game.

STARS OF THE FUTURE

NAME: Kieron Courtney Dyer
BORN: Ipswich, Suffolk, on December 29, 1978
HONOURS: None
INTERNATIONAL: England Youth, U21, 'B' and full caps
SQUAD NUMBER: 7
MOST LIKELY TO BE: England's right wing-back for the next 10 years or so. Fit as a fiddle, exciting on the ball and great pushing forward, it's his defending that lets him down at the moment. But that'll get better.

KIERON DYER

A star striker for his school team - Westbourne High in Ipswich - and for the 4th Ipswich Boys' Brigade, Kieron was thrilled when his local club, Ipswich, offered him a place as an associate schoolboy.

He joined Ipswich as a youth player and began his England career on April 29, 1996, when he lined up alongside the likes of Michael Owen and Michael Bridges in the U18 side which beat Portugal 2-1.

Dyer's senior Ipswich debut was a perfect Christmas present - it came on Boxing Day 1996 as Town romped to a 3-1 home win over Crystal Palace.

On January 3, 1997, Dyer's dream came true when he signed full pro forms with his home town club. It could only have been bettered if it had been Liverpool, the team he supported.

Kieron's first senior goal came in August 1997 against Bradford, and it was Ipswich's first goal of the season.

The impressive Kieron was called up to the England U21 squad for their fixture with Moldova on September 9, 1997. England won the game 1-0, but the real celebrations in the Dyer household began a few weeks later. Kieron was selected to play Italy away on October 10 - and he scored the only goal of the game.

Within a few months, the teenager stepped up another gear as he played for the England 'B' team on February 10, 1998. Kieron was in the side again when they beat Russia 4-1 in their very next game.

What an amazing game on March 2, 1999. Kieron scored the first in a 3-2 Ipswich win over Watford. Nothing unusual about that you might think, but it was later discovered that he had broken his leg before scoring!

He soon recovered and was back in the side before the end of the season, which ended with Ipswich in the Play-Offs and a dream call-up to the full England squad. His debut for the senior side came against Luxembourg at Wembley on September 4, 1999.

Ruud Gullit knew a good player when he saw one and signed Dyer for Newcastle on August 7, 1999, at a cost of £6m.

After a poor start to the season Newcastle came alive on September 19, in their second game under new manager Bobby Robson - who Dyer later describes as "like a father to me". The Magpies beat Sheff Wed 8-0, with Kieron scoring number five. The young hero had announced his arrival in style.

NAME: Steven George Gerrard
BORN: Huyton on May 30, 1980
HONOURS: None
INTERNATIONAL: England Youth, U21, full caps
SQUAD NUMBER: 28
MOST LIKELY TO BE: The natural successor to the likes of Paul Ince and David Batty in the England midfield. He's a highly competitive player who can also pass his way out of trouble.

STEVEN GERRARD

A Liverpool supporter through and through, as soon as he was old enough, Steven was a regular at Anfield, and his hero was Ronnie Whelan. "He made the game look easy, but really he worked so hard," said Steven. By the time he signed schoolboy forms with Liverpool, Whelan had just left to join Southend. Gerrard went on to sign professional with the Reds on February 26, 1998.

S even months later came another big day in his fledgling career, when he was picked for the England youth team for an international against the Republic of Ireland. Not only did England win 5-0, but Steven scored the second goal.

O n November 29, 1998, when Liverpool were at home to Blackburn, he made his debut as a substitute in a 2-0 victory. The very next game he was in the side from the start. A few days later, on December 8, Liverpool were at home to Celta Vigo in the UEFA Cup. They narrowly lost the tie, but Steven Gerrard won his first man of the match award after a cracking individual display.

S o impressive had his early form been that in March 1999 he was invited to train with the full England squad. There was a scare that month, though, when it was suspected that he might have a stress fracture of his back. Tests later gave him the all-clear.

O n September 3, 1999, he was called up for an important England U21 match against Luxembourg. The 5-0 win confirmed England's place at the top of their Euro 2000 group and Steven scored the first goal. A few months later, in March 2000, he starred in the U21 play-off against Yugoslavia in Spain that helped England to book their place in the finals tournament courtesy of a comfortable 3-0 victory.

H e nearly took another huge step on his career path on February 23, 2000, when England drew with Argentina at Wembley. Manager Kevin Keegan told Gerrard that he would have been making his debut but for an unlucky groin injury.

I njury struck again just as it seemed that he might be going to make his debut for England in the friendly against Brazil at Wembley on May 27, 2000. But there was some compensation, Steven did get to play his first senior international game, against the Ukraine, just three days later. It was the day of his 20th birthday and was a perfect present!

STARS OF THE FUTURE

GARETH BARRY

NAME: Gareth Barry
BORN: Hastings, East Sussex, on February 23, 1981
HONOURS: None
INTERNATIONAL: England Youth, U21 and full caps
SQUAD NUMBER: 15
MOST LIKELY TO BE: A leading figure in England's central defence. Cool, calm and confident on the ball, he has all the qualities a modern-day footballer needs. Could be England's first genuine sweeper, happy attacking and defending.

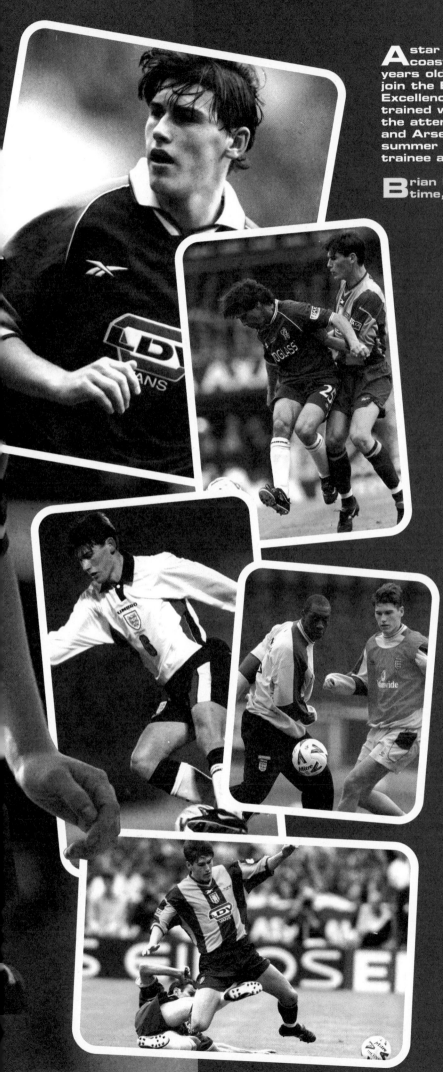

A star of schoolboy football on the south coast, happy playing against boys two years older than him, Gareth was invited to join the Brighton & Hove Albion School of Excellence. So impressive was his form that he trained with England Schoolboys, and came to the attention of clubs like Aston Villa, Chelsea and Arsenal. He tried out with Villa and in the summer of 1997 he left school and became a trainee at Villa Park.

B rian Little was the Villa manager at that time, and he gave Gareth a boost by telling him that he thought it would not be long before he was training with the first-team. In his first season as a trainee at Villa Park he not only played for England U16s, but captained the side and then went on to play for the U18 team as well.

F ollowing the departure of Brian Little, Gareth wondered if he would be back with the youth team under the new manager, but John Gregory had no hesitation in putting him into the first-team squad, and even onto the bench for a few games.

T here were big celebrations in the Barry family on February 27, 1998, when the youngster signed a five-year contract as a full-time professional with Aston Villa. His big moment on the pitch arrived when he was sent on as substitute for Ian Taylor in a 3-1 win away to Sheffield Wednesday on May 2, 1998. In the next match, against Arsenal, he was in the starting line-up and helped beat the Gunners 1-0. It was the last day of the season, and he was still only 17.

T he following campaign began at Everton, and Gareth found himself in the first-team from the start. He missed only two Premiership games all season and, on May 8, 1999, he scored his first senior goal in a 2-0 win over Nottingham Forest.

O n November 17, 1998 he made his debut for the England U21 side. They lost 1-0 to the Czech Republic, but Gareth did well and kept his place in the side.

I n March 1999 Gareth's career took another great leap forward when he was invited by then manager Glenn Hoddle to train with the Full England squad. Suddenly he found himself in practice matches with Alan Shearer, Michael Owen and other stars. He said at the time that he thought he should be asking them all for their autographs!

G areth did himself no harm when playing for Villa on May 20, 2000 in the FA Cup Final against Chelsea.

H is big break in an England shirt came on May 31, 2000, when he came on as a 74th minute sub for Phil Neville as the Ukraine were beaten 2-0 at Wembley.

Shoot

MALCOLM CHRISTIE
DERBY COUNTY

FINAL SCORE
STATS
SPECIAL

Arsenal Aston Villa Bradford Celtic Charlton Coventry Derby Everton
Ipswich Leeds Leicester Liverpool Manchester City Manchester United
Middlesbrough Newcastle Rangers Southampton Sunderland
Tottenham West Ham

Also including...
Best Of...Last Word
Shoot Interactive

ARSENAL

THEIR COMPLETE LEAGUE RECORD

P	W	D	L	F	A
3800	1686	961	1193	6301	4999

TOP SCORERS

SEASON	PLAYER	LGE GOALS
1999/2000	THIERRY HENRY	17
1998/1999	NICOLAS ANELKA	17
1997/1998	DENNIS BERGKAMP	16
1996/1997	IAN WRIGHT	23
1995/1996	IAN WRIGHT	15

(All figures correct up to summer 2000)

KICKIN' OFF

SUCCESSIVE WINS AT START OF
SEASON: 8 (1903/04)

SUCCESSIVE DEFEATS
AT START OF SEASON:
4 (1923/24)

SUCCESSIVE UNBEATEN GAMES
AT START OF SEASON:
23 (1990/91)

ON THE RUN

SUCCESSIVE GAMES
UNBEATEN:
26 (28-Apr-1980)

SUCCESSIVE GAMES WITHOUT
A WIN:
23 (28-Sep-1912)

SUCCESSIVE WINS:
10 (12-Sep-1987)

SUCCESSIVE DEFEATS:
7 (12-Feb-1977)

SUCCESSIVE DRAWS:
6 (04-Mar-1961)

SUCCESSIVE GAMES WITHOUT
SCORING:
6 (25-Feb-1987)

SUCCESSIVE GAMES
WITHOUT CONCEDING:
8 (10-Apr-1903)

HIGHS & LOWS

BIGGEST HOME WIN:
12-0 v Loughborough Town
(12-Mar-1900)

BIGGEST AWAY WIN:
7-1 v Wolves (05-Nov-1932),
6-0 v Spurs (06-Mar-1935),
7-1 v Aston Villa (14-Dec-1935)

BIGGEST HOME DEFEAT:
0-5 v Liverpool
(28-Oct-1893),
v Huddersfield
(14-Feb-1925)

BIGGEST AWAY DEFEAT:
0-8 v Loughborough Town
(12-Dec-1896)

FIRST TIME

FIRST LEAGUE GAME:
Home v Newcastle Utd
(02-Sep-1893)
RESULT: D2-2
FINAL POSITION: 9th

WIN, LOSE OR DRAW

MOST WINS (in a season):
29 (1970/71)

MOST DRAWS: 18 (1969/70)

MOST DEFEATS:
23 (1912/13), (1924/25)

GOALS

MOST GOALS SCORED
(in a season):
127 (1930/31)

FEWEST GOALS SCORED:
26 (1912/13)

MOST GOALS CONCEDED:
86 (1926/27), (1927/28)

FEWEST GOALS CONCEDED:
18 (1990/91)

MOST CLEAN SHEETS:
25 (1970/71)

FEWEST CLEAN SHEETS:
3 (1927/28)

ASTON VILLA

THEIR COMPLETE LEAGUE RECORD

P	W	D	L	F	A
3976	1686	911	1379	6646	5800

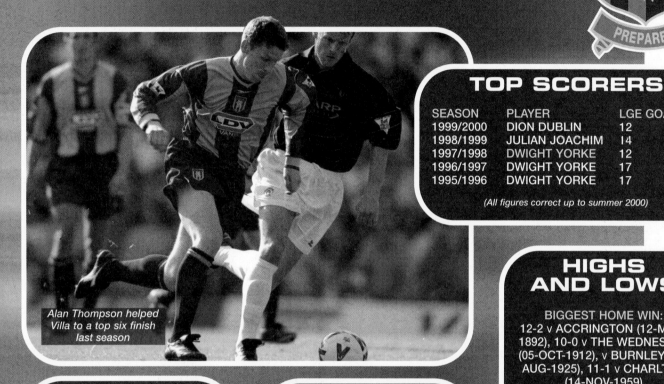

Alan Thompson helped Villa to a top six finish last season

TOP SCORERS

SEASON	PLAYER	LGE GOALS
1999/2000	DION DUBLIN	12
1998/1999	JULIAN JOACHIM	14
1997/1998	DWIGHT YORKE	12
1996/1997	DWIGHT YORKE	17
1995/1996	DWIGHT YORKE	17

(All figures correct up to summer 2000)

HIGHS AND LOWS

BIGGEST HOME WIN:
12-2 v ACCRINGTON (12-MAR-1892), 10-0 v THE WEDNESDAY (05-OCT-1912), v BURNLEY (29-AUG-1925), 11-1 v CHARLTON (14-NOV-1959)

BIGGEST AWAY WIN: 6-0 v MAN UTD (14-MAR-1914), v OLDHAM (27-NOV-1971)

BIGGEST HOME DEFEAT: 0-7 v WEST BROM (19-OCT-1935)

BIGGEST AWAY DEFEAT: 0-7 v BLACKBURN (19-OCT-1889), v EVERTON (04-JAN-1890), v MAN UTD (08-MAR-1950), v MAN UTD (24-OCT-1964), (1899/1900), (1909/10), (1980/81)

ON THE RUN

SUCCESSIVE GAMES UNBEATEN: 15 (16-JAN-1897), (18-MAR-1909), (12-MAR 1949)

SUCCESSIVE GAMES WITHOUT A WIN: 12 (10-NOV-1973), (27-DEC-1986)

SUCCESSIVE WINS: 9 (22-MAR-1897), (15-OCT-1910)

SUCCESSIVE DEFEATS: 11 (23-MAR-1963)

SUCCESSIVE DRAWS: 6 (12-SEP-1981)

SUCCESSIVE GAMES WITHOUT SCORING: 5 (23-DEC-1961), (01-MAR-1989), (11 JAN-1992), (29-JAN-1992)

SUCCESSIVE GAMES WITHOUT CONCEDING: 7 (27-OCT-1923)

WIN, LOSE OR DRAW

MOST WINS (IN A SEASON): 32 (1971/72)

MOST DRAWS: 17 (1975/76)

MOST DEFEATS: 24 (1966/67)

KICKIN' OFF

SUCCESSIVE WINS AT START OF SEASON: 4 (1891/92), (1897/98), (1900/01), (1930/31)

SUCCESSIVE DEFEATS AT START OF SEASON: 3 (1964/65), (1982/83), (1986/87)

SUCCESSIVE UNBEATEN GAMES AT START OF SEASON: 11 (1932/33)

GOALS

MOST GOALS SCORED (IN A SEASON): 128 (1930/31)
FEWEST GOALS SCORED: 36 (1969/70)
MOST GOALS CONCEDED: 110 (1935/36)
FEWEST GOALS CONCEDED: 32 (1971/72), (1974/75)
MOST CLEAN SHEETS: 26 (1971/72)
FEWEST CLEAN SHEETS: 1 (1888/89)

FIRST TIME

FIRST LEAGUE GAME: AWAY v WOLVES (08-SEP-1888)
RESULT: DREW 1-1
FINAL POSITION: 2ND

BRADFORD

THEIR COMPLETE LEAGUE RECORD

P	W	D	L	F	A
3806	1388	1025	1393	5378	5345

THE BANTAMS

TOP SCORERS

SEASON	PLAYER	LGE GOALS
1999/2000	DEAN WINDASS	10
1998/1999	LEE MILLS	24
1997/1998	ROB STEINER/EDINHO	10
1996/1997	OLE SUNDGOT	6
1995/1996	MARK STALLARD	9

(All figures correct up to summer 2000)

KICKIN' OFF

SUCCESSIVE WINS AT START OF SEASON:
5 (1932/33)

SUCCESSIVE DEFEATS AT START OF SEASON:
5 (1949/50)

SUCCESSIVE UNBEATEN GAMES AT START OF SEASON:
8 (1954/55), (1979/80)

ON THE RUN

SUCCESSIVE GAMES UNBEATEN:
21 (11-JAN-1969)

SUCCESSIVE GAMES WITHOUT A WIN: 16 (28-AUG-1948)

SUCCESSIVE WINS:
10 (26-NOV-1983)

SUCCESSIVE DEFEATS:
8 (21-JAN-1933)

SUCCESSIVE DRAWS:
6 (30-JAN-1976)

SUCCESSIVE GAMES WITHOUT SCORING:
7 (18-APR-1925), (15-APR-1995)

SUCCESSIVE GAMES WITHOUT CONCEDING:
5 (22-APR-1905), (30-OCT-1909), (28-FEB-1911), (06-MAR-1929), (29-AUG-1953), (16-JAN-1954)

HIGHS AND LOWS

BIGGEST HOME WIN:
11-1 v ROTHERHAM UNITED
(25-AUG-1928)

BIGGEST AWAY WIN:
8-2 v ASHINGTON (13-OCT-1928),
6-0 v NEW BRIGHTON
(03-FEB-1951)

BIGGEST HOME DEFEAT:
1-7 v STOCKPORT COUNTY
(18-SEP-1965)

BIGGEST AWAY DEFEAT:
0-8 v MANCHESTER CITY
(07-MAY-1927), 1-9 v
COLCHESTER
UTD (30-DEC-1961)

FIRST TIME

FIRST LEAGUE GAME:
AWAY v GRIMSBY TOWN
(01-SEP-1903)
RESULT: LOST 0-2
FINAL POSITION: 10TH

WIN, LOSE OR DRAW

MOST WINS (IN A SEASON):
28 (1984/85)

MOST DRAWS:
20 (1968/69)

MOST DEFEATS:
26 (1926/27), (1964/65)

GOALS

MOST GOALS SCORED
(IN A SEASON):
128 (1928/29)

FEWEST GOALS SCORED:
35 (1923/24)

MOST GOALS CONCEDED:
94 (1936/37), (1965/66)

FEWEST GOALS CONCEDED:
40 (1913/14)

MOST CLEAN SHEETS:
20 (1953/54)

FEWEST CLEAN SHEETS:
3 (1960/61)

CELTIC

THEIR LEAGUE RECORD LAST SEASON

P	W	D	L	F	A
36	21	6	9	90	38

Celtic were rarely on the ball against Rangers last season

TOP SCORERS

SEASON	PLAYER	LGE GOALS
1999/2000	MARK VIDUKA	25
1990/1999	HENRIK LARSSON	29
1997/1998	HENRIK LARSSON	16
1996/1997	JORGE CADETE	25
1995/1996	PIERRE V. HOOIJDONK	24

(All figures correct up to summer 2000)

CLUB HONOURS

LEAGUE CHAMPIONS:
36 TIMES INCLUDING PREMIER
WINNERS IN: (1976/77, 1978/79,
1980/81, 1981/82, 1985/86,
1987/88, 1997/98)

SCOTTISH CUP WINNERS:
30 TIMES

SCOTTISH CUP RUNNERS-UP:
17 TIMES

SCOTTISH LEAGUE CUP
WINNERS:
(1956/57, 1957/58, 1965/66,
1966/67, 1967/68, 1968/69,
1969/70, 1974/75, 1982/83,
1997/98, 1999/2000)

SCOTTISH LEAGUE CUP
RUNNERS-UP:
10 TIMES

EUROPEAN CUP WINNERS:
(1966/67)

EUROPEAN CUP RUNNERS-UP:
(1969/70)

EUROPEAN CUP-WINNERS' CUP
WINNERS:
NONE

EUROPEAN CUP-WINNERS' CUP
RUNNERS-UP:
NONE

UEFA CUP WINNERS:
NONE

UEFA CUP RUNNERS-UP:
NONE

MOST CAPPED PLAYER

PADDY BONNER 80 REPUBLIC
OF IRELAND

DEBUT v POLAND IN 1981,
LAST APPEARANCE v BOLIVIA
1996

HIGHS AND LOWS

BIGGEST HOME WIN:
11-0 v DUNDEE
(26-OCT-1895)

BIGGEST AWAY WIN:
8-0 v HAMILTON
(5-NOV-1988)

BIGGEST HOME DEFEAT:
1-4 v AYR UNITED
(11-NOV-1922)

BIGGEST AWAY DEFEAT:
0-8 v MOTHERWELL
(30-APRIL-1937)

RECORD BREAKERS

MOST LEAGUE GOALS SCORED
BY A PLAYER (IN A SEASON):
JAMES McGRORY (1935/36) 50

MOST GOALS SCORED BY A
PLAYER OVERALL:
JAMES McGRORY (1922/39) 397

BIGGEST FEE PAID OUT BY THE
CLUB FOR A PLAYER
£5.5 MILLION TO WEST HAM
UNITED FOR EYAL BERKOVIC IN
JULY 1999

BIGGEST FEE RECEIVED BY THE
CLUB FOR A PLAYER:
£7 MILLION FROM LEEDS FOR
MARK VIDUKA IN JUNE 2000

FIRST TIME

FIRST LEAGUE GAME:
HOME v RENTON
(16-AUG-1890)
RESULT: LOST 1-4
FINAL POSITION: 3RD

CHARLTON

THEIR COMPLETE LEAGUE RECORD

P	W	D	L	F	A
3062	1121	766	1175	4493	4705

TOP SCORERS

SEASON	PLAYER	LGE GOALS
1999/2000	ANDY HUNT	24
1998/1999	CLIVE MENDONCA	8
1997/1998	CLIVE MENDONCA	23
1996/1997	CARL LEABURN	
	DAVID WHYTE	7
1995/1996	CARL LEABURN	9

(All figures correct up to summer 2000)

Shaun Newton helped Charlton to promotion last season

KICKIN' OFF

SUCCESSIVE WINS AT START OF SEASON: 4 (1992/93)

SUCCESSIVE DEFEATS AT START OF SEASON:
5 (1956/57)

SUCCESSIVE UNBEATEN GAMES AT START OF SEASON:
12 (1927/28)

ON THE RUN

SUCCESSIVE GAMES UNBEATEN:
15 (04-OCT-1980)

SUCCESSIVE GAMES WITHOUT A WIN:
16 (26-FEB-1955)

SUCCESSIVE WINS:
12 (26-DEC-1999)

SUCCESSIVE DEFEATS:
10 (11-APR-1990)

SUCCESSIVE DRAWS:
6 (13-DEC-1992)

SUCCESSIVE GAMES WITHOUT SCORING:
5 (06-SEP-1922)

SUCCESSIVE GAMES WITHOUT CONCEDING:
7 (22-DEC-1923)

HIGHS AND LOWS

BIGGEST HOME WIN:
8-1 v MIDDLESBROUGH
(12-SEP-1953)

BIGGEST AWAY WIN:
6-1 v LUTON TOWN
(10-FEB-1962)

BIGGEST HOME DEFEAT:
0-7 v EVERTON
(07-FEB-1931)

BIGGEST AWAY DEFEAT:
1-11 v ASTON VILLA
(14-NOV-1959)

FIRST TIME

FIRST LEAGUE GAME:
HOME v EXETER CITY
(27-AUG-1921)
RESULT: WON 1-0
FINAL POSITION: 16TH

WIN, LOSE OR DRAW

MOST WINS (IN A SEASON):
27 (1934/35), (1999/00)
MOST DRAWS:
20 (1995/96)
MOST DEFEATS:
29 (1956/57)

GOALS

MOST GOALS SCORED
(IN A SEASON):
107 (1957/58)

FEWEST GOALS SCORED:
31 (1989/90)

MOST GOALS CONCEDED:
120 (1956/57)

FEWEST GOALS CONCEDED:
44 (1980/81)

MOST CLEAN SHEETS:
20 (1980/81)

FEWEST CLEAN SHEETS:
2 (1956/57)

CHELSEA

THEIR COMPLETE LEAGUE RECORD

P	W	D	L	F	A
3462	1337	916	1209	5197	5009

French ace Marcel Desailly - one of the many foreign stars who have played for Chelsea

TOP SCORERS

SEASON	PLAYER	LGE GOALS
1999/2000	TORE ANDRE FLO	
	GUSTAVO POYET	10
1998/1999	GIANFRANCO ZOLA	13
1997/1998	GIANLUCA VIALLI	
	TORE ANDRE FLO	11
1996/1997	GIANLUCA VIALLI	9
1995/1996	JOHN SPENCER	10

(All figures correct up to summer 2000)

GOALS

MOST GOALS SCORED (IN A SEASON):
98 (1960/61)
FEWEST GOALS SCORED:
31 (1923/24)
MOST GOALS CONCEDED:
100 (1960/61)
FEWEST GOALS CONCEDED:
30 (1998/99)
MOST CLEAN SHEETS:
19 (1925/26)
FEWEST CLEAN SHEETS:
1 (1960/61)

HIGHS AND LOWS

BIGGEST HOME WIN:
7-0 v BURSLEM PORT VALE
(03-MAR-1906), 9-2 v GLOSSOP
(01-SEP-1906), 7-0 v LINCOLN
CITY (29-OCT-1910), v
PORTSMOUTH (21-MAY-1963)

BIGGEST AWAY WIN:
7-0 v WALSALL (04-FEB-1989)

BIGGEST HOME DEFEAT:
0-6 v NOTTS COUNTY
(09-FEB-1924)

BIGGEST AWAY DEFEAT:
1-8 v WOLVERHAMPTON W.
(26-SEP-1953), 0-7 v LEEDS UTD
(07-OCT-1967), v NOTTINGHAM
FOREST (20-APR-1991)

ON THE RUN

SUCCESSIVE GAMES
UNBEATEN:
27 (29-OCT-1988)

SUCCESSIVE GAMES
WITHOUT A WIN:
21 (03-NOV-1987)

SUCCESSIVE WINS:
8 (06-OCT-1927), (15-MAR-1989)

SUCCESSIVE DEFEATS:
7 (01-NOV-1952)

SUCCESSIVE DRAWS:
6 (20-AUG-1969)

SUCCESSIVE GAMES
WITHOUT SCORING:
9 (14-MAR-1981)

SUCCESSIVE GAMES
WITHOUT CONCEDING:
9 (04-NOV-1905)

FIRST TIME

FIRST LEAGUE GAME:
AWAY v STOCKPORT COUNTY
(02-SEP-1905)
RESULT: LOST 0-1
FINAL POSITION: 3RD

KICKIN' OFF

SUCCESSIVE WINS AT START OF
SEASON: 6 (1928/29)
SUCCESSIVE DEFEATS AT START
OF SEASON:
3 (1907/08), (1912/13), (1973/74)
SUCCESSIVE UNBEATEN GAMES
AT START OF SEASON:
14 (1925/26)

WIN, LOSE OR DRAW

MOST WINS (IN A SEASON):
29 (1988/89)
MOST DRAWS: 18 (1922/23)
MOST DEFEATS: 27 (1978/79)

COVENTRY

THEIR COMPLETE LEAGUE RECORD

P	W	D	L	F	A
3122	1116	814	1192	4456	4568

TOP SCORERS

SEASON	PLAYER	LGE GOALS
1999/2000	ROBBIE KEANE	12
1998/1999	NOEL WHELAN	10
1997/1998	DION DUBLIN	18
1996/1997	DION DUBLIN	14
1995/1996	DION DUBLIN	14

(All figures correct up to summer 2000)

Youssef Chippo - one of the stars of the season for Coventry in 2000

KICKIN' OFF

SUCCESSIVE WINS AT START OF SEASON:
5 (1964/65)

SUCCESSIVE DEFEATS AT START OF SEASON:
9 (1919/20)

SUCCESSIVE UNBEATEN GAMES AT START OF SEASON:
15 (1937/38)

ON THE RUN

SUCCESSIVE GAMES UNBEATEN:
25 (26-NOV-1966)

SUCCESSIVE GAMES WITHOUT A WIN:
19 (30-AUG-1919)

SUCCESSIVE WINS:
6 (20-APR-1954), (25-APR-1964)

SUCCESSIVE DEFEATS:
9 (30-AUG-1919)

SUCCESSIVE DRAWS:
6 (28-SEP-1996)

SUCCESSIVE GAMES WITHOUT SCORING:
11 (11-OCT-1919)

SUCCESSIVE GAMES WITHOUT CONCEDING:
6 (28-APR-1934)

HIGHS AND LOWS

BIGGEST HOME WIN:
9-0 v BRISTOL CITY
(28-APR-1934)

BIGGEST AWAY WIN:
7-0 v ABERDARE ATHLETIC
(18-APR-1927)

BIGGEST HOME DEFEAT:
0-5 v TOTTENHAM HOTSPUR
(30-AUG-1919), v EVERTON
(27-SEP-1980), 1-6 v LIVERPOOL
(05-MAY-1990)

BIGGEST AWAY DEFEAT:
1-9 v MILLWALL (19-NOV-1927),
2-10 v NORWICH CITY
(15-MAR-1930)

FIRST TIME

FIRST LEAGUE GAME:
HOME v TOTTENHAM HOTSPUR
(30-AUG-1919)
RESULT: LOST 0-5
FINAL POSITION: 20TH

WIN, LOSE OR DRAW

MOST WINS (IN A SEASON): 24
(1935/36), (1958/59)

MOST DRAWS: 17 (1962/63)

MOST DEFEATS: 22 (1919/20),
(1924/25), (1927/28), (1951/52),
(1984/85)

GOALS

MOST GOALS SCORED
(IN A SEASON):
108 (1931/32)

FEWEST GOALS SCORED:
35 (1919/20), (1991/92)

MOST GOALS CONCEDED:
97 (1931/32)

FEWEST GOALS CONCEDED:
38 (1970/71)

MOST CLEAN SHEETS:
18 (1938/39), (1958/59)

FEWEST CLEAN SHEETS:
5 (1971/72)

DERBY

THEIR COMPLETE LEAGUE RECORD

P	W	D	L	F	A
4004	1581	962	1461	6335	5964

DERBY COUNTY

TOP SCORERS

SEASON	PLAYER	LGE GOALS
1999/2000	RORY DELAP	8
1998/1999	PAULO WANCHOPE	
	DEON BURTON	9
1997/1998	PAULO WANCHOPE	13
1996/1997	DEAN STURRIDGE	11
1995/1996	DEAN STURRIDGE	20

HIGHS AND LOWS

BIGGEST HOME WIN:
9-0 v WOLVES (10-JAN-1891), v
THE WEDNESDAY (21-JAN-1899)

BIGGEST AWAY WIN:
8-0 v BRISTOL CITY (29-SEP-1923)

BIGGEST HOME DEFEAT:
1-7 v MAN CITY (29-JAN-1938),
v MIDDLESBRO (29-AUG-1959),
v LIVERPOOL (23-MAR-1991)

BIGGEST AWAY DEFEAT:
0-8 v BLACKBURN (03-JAN-1891),
v SUNDERLAND (01-SEP-1894)

ON THE RUN

SUCCESSIVE GAMES
UNBEATEN:
22 (08-MAR-1969)

SUCCESSIVE GAMES
WITHOUT A WIN:
20 (15-DEC-1990)

SUCCESSIVE WINS: 9
(15-MAR-1969)

SUCCESSIVE DEFEATS:
8 (29-SEP-1888), (17-APR-1965),
(12-DEC-1987)

SUCCESSIVE DRAWS:
6 (26-MAR-1927)

SUCCESSIVE GAMES WITHOUT
SCORING:
8 (30-OCT-1920)

SUCCESSIVE GAMES WITHOUT
CONCEDING:
6 (08-APR-1912)

(All figures correct up to summer 2000)

GOALS

MOST GOALS SCORED
(IN A SEASON): 111 (1956/57)

FEWEST GOALS SCORED:
32 (1920/21)

MOST GOALS CONCEDED:
90 (1936/37)

FEWEST GOALS CONCEDED:
28 (1911/12)

MOST CLEAN SHEETS:
23 (1971/72)

FEWEST CLEAN SHEETS:
1 (1890/91)

FIRST TIME

FIRST LEAGUE GAME:
AWAY v BOLTON WANDERERS
(08-SEP-1888)
RESULT: WON 6-3
FINAL POSITION: 10TH

WIN, LOSE OR DRAW

MOST WINS (IN A SEASON):
28 (1955/56)

MOST DRAWS:
19 (1976/77), (1982/83)

MOST DEFEATS:
26 (1954/55)

KICKIN' OFF

SUCCESSIVE WINS AT START OF
SEASON: 5 (1905/06)

SUCCESSIVE DEFEATS AT START
OF SEASON:
4 (1899/1900), (1965/66)

SUCCESSIVE UNBEATEN GAMES
AT START OF SEASON:
16 (1948/49)

EVERTON
THEIR COMPLETE LEAGUE RECORD

P	W	D	L	F	A
3964	1634	976	1354	6407	5623

TOP SCORERS

SEASON	PLAYER	LGE GOALS
1999/2000	KEVIN CAMPBELL	12
1998/1999	KEVIN CAMPBELL	9
1997/1998	DUNCAN FERGUSON	11
1996/1997	DUNCAN FERGUSON	10
1995/1996	ANDREI KANCHELSKIS	16

(All figures correct up to summer 2000)

Nick Barmby's form for Everton won him a place in the England squad for Euro 2000

KICKIN' OFF

SUCCESSIVE WINS AT START OF SEASON:
8 (1894/95)

SUCCESSIVE DEFEATS AT START OF SEASON:
6 (1958/59)

SUCCESSIVE UNBEATEN GAMES AT START OF SEASON:
19 (1978/79)

HIGHS AND LOWS

BIGGEST HOME WIN:
8-0 v STOKE (02-NOV-1889), 9-1 v MANCHESTER CITY (03 SEP-1906), 9-1 v PLYMOUTH ARGYLE (27-DEC-1930), 8-0 v SOUTHAMPTON (20-NOV-1971)

BIGGEST AWAY WIN:
7-0 v CHARLTON ATHLETIC (07-FEB-1931)

BIGGEST HOME DEFEAT:
0-6 v NEWCASTLE UTD (26-OCT-1912)

BIGGEST AWAY DEFEAT:
0-7 v SUNDERLAND (26-DEC-1934), 0-7 v WOLVES (22-FEB-1939), 0-7 v PORTSMOUTH (10-SEP-1949)

WIN, LOSE OR DRAW

MOST WINS (IN A SEASON):
29 (1969/70)

MOST DRAWS:
18 (1925/26), (1971/72), (1974/75)

MOST DEFEATS:
22 (1950/51), (1993/94)

ON THE RUN

SUCCESSIVE GAMES UNBEATEN:
20 (29-APR-1978)

SUCCESSIVE GAMES WITHOUT A WIN:
14 (06-MAR-1937)

SUCCESSIVE WINS:
12 (24-MAR-1894)

SUCCESSIVE DEFEATS:
6 (06-FEB-1897), (10-APR-1929), (05-MAR-1930), (29-MAR-1958), (23-AUG-1958), (04-NOV-1972)

SUCCESSIVE DRAWS:
5 (15-OCT-1921), (05-OCT-1974), (04-MAY-1977)

SUCCESSIVE GAMES WITHOUT SCORING:
6 (03-MAR-1951)

SUCCESSIVE GAMES WITHOUT CONCEDING:
7 (01-NOV-1994), (06-MAY-1995)

FIRST TIME

FIRST LEAGUE GAME:
HOME v ACCRINGTON (08-SEP-1888)
RESULT: WON 2-1
FINAL POSITION: 8TH

GOALS

MOST GOALS SCORED (IN A SEASON):
121 (1930/31)

FEWEST GOALS SCORED:
37 (1971/72)

MOST GOALS CONCEDED:
92 (1929/30)

FEWEST GOALS CONCEDED:
27 (1987/88)

MOST CLEAN SHEETS:
21 (1969/70)

FEWEST CLEAN SHEETS:
2 (1888/89)

NIL SATIS NISI OPTIMUM

IPSWICH

THEIR COMPLETE LEAGUE RECORD

P	W	D	L	F	A
2372	972	587	813	3548	3256

TOP SCORERS

SEASON	PLAYER	LGE GOALS
1999/2000	DAVID JOHNSON	22
1998/1999	DAVID JOHNSON	14
1997/1998	DAVID JOHNSON	20
1996/1997	PAUL MASON	12
1995/1996	IAN MARSHALL	19

(All figures correct up to summer 2000)

KICKIN' OFF

SUCCESSIVE WINS AT START OF SEASON:
4 (1953/54), (1974/75)

SUCCESSIVE DEFEATS AT START OF SEASON:
3 (1949/50), (1956/57)

SUCCESSIVE UNBEATEN GAMES AT START OF SEASON:
14 (1980/81)

WIN, LOSE OR DRAW

MOST WINS (IN A SEASON):
27 (1953/54)

MOST DRAWS: 18 (1990/91)

MOST DEFEATS: 29 (1994/95)

HIGHS AND LOWS

BIGGEST HOME WIN:
7-0 v PORTSMOUTH (07-NOV-1964), 7-0 v SOUTHAMPTON (02-FEB-1974), 7-0 v WEST BROMWICH ALB. (06-NOV-1976)

BIGGEST AWAY WIN:
6-0 v NOTTS COUNTY (25-SEP-1982) 6-0 v SWINDON TOWN (03-APR-1999)

BIGGEST HOME DEFEAT:
1-6 V MILLWALL (21-MAR-1953), 2-7 v MANCHESTER UTD (03-SEP-1963)

BIGGEST AWAY DEFEAT:
1-10 v FULHAM (26-DEC-1963), 0-9 v MAN UTD (04-MAR-1995)

ON THE RUN

SUCCESSIVE GAMES UNBEATEN:
23 (08-DEC-1979)

SUCCESSIVE GAMES WITHOUT A WIN:
21 (28-AUG-1963)

SUCCESSIVE WINS:
8 (23-SEP-1953)

SUCCESSIVE DEFEATS:
10 (04-SEP-1954)

SUCCESSIVE DRAWS:
7 (10-NOV-1990)

SUCCESSIVE GAMES WITHOUT SCORING:
7 (28-FEB-1995)

SUCCESSIVE GAMES WITHOUT CONCEDING:
9 (14-MAR-1998)

GOALS

MOST GOALS SCORED (IN A SEASON):
106 (1955/56)

FEWEST GOALS SCORED:
32 (1985/86)

MOST GOALS CONCEDED:
121 (1963/64)

FEWEST GOALS CONCEDED:
32 (1998/99)

MOST CLEAN SHEETS:
25 (1998/99)

FEWEST CLEAN SHEETS:
3 (1994/95)

FIRST TIME

FIRST LEAGUE GAME:
HOME v SOUTHEND UTD (27-AUG-1938)
RESULT: WON 4-2
FINAL POSITION: 7TH

LEEDS

THEIR COMPLETE LEAGUE RECORD

P	W	D	L	F	A
3052	1269	798	985	4595	4019

TOP SCORERS

SEASON	PLAYER	LGE GOALS
1999/2000	MICHAEL BRIDGES	19
1998/1999	JF HASSELBAINK	18
1997/1998	JF HASSELBAINK	16
1996/1997	DEANE/ SHARPE	5
1995/1996	TONY YEBOAH	12

(All figures correct up to summer 2000)

Leeds qualified for the Champions League after finishing third in the Premiership in 2000

KICKIN' OFF

SUCCESSIVE WINS AT START OF SEASON:
7 (1973/74)

SUCCESSIVE DEFEATS AT START OF SEASON:
3 (1936/37)

SUCCESSIVE UNBEATEN GAMES AT START OF SEASON:
29 (1973/74)

HIGHS AND LOWS

BIGGEST HOME WIN:
8-0 v LEICESTER CITY
(07-APR-1934)

BIGGEST AWAY WIN:
5-0 v BURNLEY
(21-NOV-1931),
5-0 v FULHAM (06-JAN 1968),
6-1 v SHEFFIELD WED.
(12-JAN-1992),
5-0 v SWINDON TOWN
(07-MAY 1994)

BIGGEST HOME DEFEAT:
0-5 v ARSENAL (08-NOV-1980)

BIGGEST AWAY DEFEAT:
1-8 v STOKE CITY (27-AUG-1934)

WIN, LOSE OR DRAW

MOST WINS (IN A SEASON):
27 (1968/69), (1970/71)

MOST DRAWS: 21 (1982/83)

MOST DEFEATS: 30 (1946/47)

ON THE RUN

SUCCESSIVE GAMES UNBEATEN:
34 (26-OCT-1968)

SUCCESSIVE GAMES WITHOUT A WIN:
17 (01-FEB-1947)

SUCCESSIVE WINS:
9 (26-SEP-1931)

SUCCESSIVE DEFEATS:
6 (26-APR-1947), 6 (6-APR-1996)

SUCCESSIVE DRAWS:
5 (09-APR-1962)

SUCCESSIVE GAMES WITHOUT SCORING:
6 (30-JAN-1982)

SUCCESSIVE GAMES WITHOUT CONCEDING:
9 (03-MAR-1928)

GOALS

MOST GOALS SCORED
(IN A SEASON):
98 (1927/28)

FEWEST GOALS SCORED:
28 (1996/97)

MOST GOALS CONCEDED:
92 (1934/35), (1959/60)

FEWEST GOALS CONCEDED:
26 (1968/69)

MOST CLEAN SHEETS:
24 (1968/69), (1970/71)

FEWEST CLEAN SHEETS:
3 (1926/27), (1946/47)

FIRST TIME

FIRST LEAGUE GAME:
AWAY v PORT VALE
(28-AUG-1920)
RESULT: LOST 0-2
FINAL POSITION: 14TH

LEICESTER

THEIR COMPLETE LEAGUE RECORD

P	W	D	L	F	A
3860	1432	980	1448	5892	5999

TOP SCORERS

SEASON	PLAYER	LGE GOALS
1999/2000	TONY COTTEE	13
1998/1999	TONY COTTEE	10
1997/1998	EMILE HESKEY	10
1996/1997	STEVE CLARIDGE	12
1995/1996	IWAN ROBERTS	19

(All figures correct up to summer 2000)

KICKIN' OFF

SUCCESSIVE WINS AT START OF SEASON:
3 (1899/1900), (1906/07), (1922/23)

SUCCESSIVE DEFEATS AT START OF SEASON:
6 (1983/84)

SUCCESSIVE UNBEATEN GAMES AT START OF SEASON:
11 (1899/1900)

WIN, LOSE OR DRAW

MOST WINS (IN A SEASON):
25 (1956/57)

MOST DRAWS:
19 (1975/76)

MOST DEFEATS:
25 (1913/14), (1977/78), (1994/95)

HIGHS AND LOWS

BIGGEST HOME WIN:
10-0 v PORTSMOUTH
(20-OCT-1928)

BIGGEST AWAY WIN:
5-0 v BURTON SWIFTS (02-MAR-1895), 6-1 v LUTON TOWN (14-JAN-1899), 5-0 v CHARLTON ATHLETIC (28-MAR-1970)

BIGGEST HOME DEFEAT:
0-6 v DERBY COUNTY (28-DEC-1914), 0-6 v WEST HAM UTD (15-FEB-1923)

BIGGEST AWAY DEFEAT:
0-12 v NOTTINGHAM FOREST (21-APR-1909)

ON THE RUN

SUCCESSIVE GAMES UNBEATEN:
19 (06-FEB-1971)

SUCCESSIVE GAMES WITHOUT A WIN:
18 (12-APR-1975)

SUCCESSIVE WINS:
7 (15-FEB-1908), (24-JAN-1925), (26-DEC-1962), (28 FEB-1993)

SUCCESSIVE DEFEATS:
7 (28-NOV-1931), (28-AUG-1990)

SUCCESSIVE DRAWS:
6 (21-APR-1973), (21-AUG-1976)

SUCCESSIVE GAMES WITHOUT SCORING:
7 (21-NOV-1987)

SUCCESSIVE GAMES WITHOUT CONCEDING:
7 (14-FEB-1920)

GOALS

MOST GOALS SCORED (IN A SEASON):
109 (1956/57)

FEWEST GOALS SCORED:
26 (1977/78)

MOST GOALS CONCEDED:
112 (1957/58)

FEWEST GOALS CONCEDED:
30 (1970/71)

MOST CLEAN SHEETS:
23 (1970/71)

FEWEST CLEAN SHEETS:
2 (1908/09)

FIRST TIME

FIRST LEAGUE GAME:
AWAY v GRIMSBY TOWN
(01-SEP-1894)
RESULT: LOST 3-4
FINAL POSITION: 4TH

LIVERPOOL FOOTBALL CLUB

EST. 1892

LIVERPOOL
THEIR COMPLETE LEAGUE RECORD

P	W	D	L	F	A
3840	1795	934	1111	6576	4866

TOP SCORERS

SEASON	PLAYER	LGE GOALS
1999/2000	MICHAEL OWEN	11
1998/1999	MICHAEL OWEN	17
1997/1998	MICHAEL OWEN	18
1996/1997	ROBBIE FOWLER	18
1995/1996	ROBBIE FOWLER	28

(All figures correct up to summer 2000)

Emile Heskey - a £11 million buy from Leicester last season

KICKIN' OFF

SUCCESSIVE WINS AT START OF SEASON:
8 (1990/91)

SUCCESSIVE DEFEATS AT START OF SEASON:
8 (1899/00)

SUCCESSIVE UNBEATEN GAMES AT START OF SEASON:
29 (1987/88)

ON THE RUN

SUCCESSIVE GAMES UNBEATEN:
31 (04-MAY-1987)

SUCCESSIVE GAMES WITHOUT A WIN:
14 (12-DEC-1953)

SUCCESSIVE WINS:
12 (21-APR-1990)

SUCCESSIVE DEFEATS:
9 (29-APR-1899)

SUCCESSIVE DRAWS:
6 (19-FEB-1975)

SUCCESSIVE GAMES WITHOUT SCORING:
5 (22-DEC-1906), (03-JAN-1948), (18-DEC-1971), (01-SEP-1993), (21-APR-2000)

SUCCESSIVE GAMES WITHOUT CONCEDING:
8 (30-DEC-1922)

HIGHS AND LOWS

BIGGEST HOME WIN:
10-1 v ROTHERHAM TOWN (18-FEB-1896), 9-0 v CRYSTAL PALACE (12-SEP-1989)

BIGGEST AWAY WIN:
7-0 v BURTON SWIFTS (29-FEB-1896) 7-0 v CREWE ALEXANDRA (28-MAR-1896)

BIGGEST HOME DEFEAT:
0-6 v SUNDERLAND (19-APR-1930)

BIGGEST AWAY DEFEAT:
0-8 v HUDDERSFIELD TOWN (10-NOV-1934), 1-9 v BIRMINGHAM (11-DEC-1954)

FIRST TIME

FIRST LEAGUE GAME:
AWAY v MIDDLESBROUGH (02-SEP-1893)
RESULT: WON 2-0
FINAL POSITION: 1ST

WIN, LOSE OR DRAW

MOST WINS (IN A SEASON):
30 (1978/79)

MOST DRAWS:
19 (1951/52)

MOST DEFEATS:
23 (1953/54)

GOALS

MOST GOALS SCORED (IN A SEASON):
106 (1895/96)

FEWEST GOALS SCORED:
42 (1901/02), (1970/71)

MOST GOALS CONCEDED:
97 (1953/54)

FEWEST GOALS CONCEDED:
16 (1978/79)

MOST CLEAN SHEETS:
28 (1978/79)

FEWEST CLEAN SHEETS:
4 (1894/95), (1927/28), (1931/32), (1954/55)

MAN CITY

THEIR COMPLETE LEAGUE RECORD

P	W	D	L	F	A
3906	1585	953	1368	6371	5726

M.C.F.C.
Superbia In Proelio ™

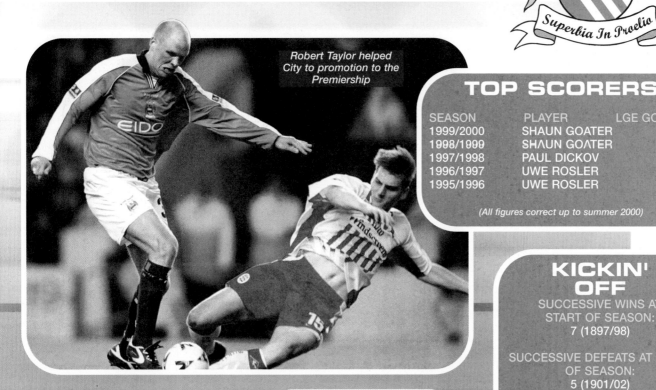

Robert Taylor helped City to promotion to the Premiership

TOP SCORERS

SEASON	PLAYER	LGE GOALS
1999/2000	SHAUN GOATER	23
1998/1999	SHAUN GOATER	18
1997/1998	PAUL DICKOV	9
1996/1997	UWE ROSLER	15
1995/1996	UWE ROSLER	9

(All figures correct up to summer 2000)

KICKIN' OFF

SUCCESSIVE WINS AT START OF SEASON:
7 (1897/98)

SUCCESSIVE DEFEATS AT START OF SEASON:
5 (1901/02)

SUCCESSIVE UNBEATEN GAMES AT START OF SEASON:
11 (1914/15)

WIN, LOSE OR DRAW

MOST WINS (IN A SEASON):
26 (1946/47), (1967/68), (1999/00)

MOST DRAWS:
18 (1993/94)

MOST DEFEATS:
22 (1959/60), (1997/98)

HIGHS AND LOWS

BIGGEST HOME WIN:
10-0 v DARWEN (18-FEB-1899)

BIGGEST AWAY WIN:
7-1 v DERBY COUNTY (29-JAN-1938), 9-3 v TRANMERE ROVERS (26-DEC-1938)

BIGGEST HOME DEFEAT:
2-7 v WEST BROMWICH ALB. (01-JAN-1934), 1-6 v MIDDLESBROUGH (09-MAR-1938), 1-6 v MILLWALL (17-SEP-1938), 1-6 v BLACKPOOL (23-APR-1955), 1-6 v WEST HAM UTD (08-SEP-1962),

BIGGEST AWAY DEFEAT:
2-10 v SMALL HEATH (17 MARCH 1894)

ON THE RUN

SUCCESSIVE GAMES UNBEATEN:
22 (26-DEC-1936), (16-NOV-1946)

SUCCESSIVE GAMES WITHOUT A WIN:
17 (26-DEC-1979)

SUCCESSIVE WINS:
9 (08-APR-1912)

SUCCESSIVE DEFEATS:
6 (10-SEP-1910), (12-SEP-1956), (30-MAR-1959), (05-NOV-1960), (09-MAR-1963)

SUCCESSIVE DRAWS:
6 (05-APR-1913)

SUCCESSIVE GAMES WITHOUT SCORING:
6 (30-JAN-1971)

SUCCESSIVE GAMES WITHOUT CONCEDING:
5 (20-MAR-1915), (28-DEC-1946), (23-FEB-1985)

GOALS

MOST GOALS SCORED (IN A SEASON):
108 (1926/27)

FEWEST GOALS SCORED:
36 (1949/50), (1986/87)

MOST GOALS CONCEDED:
102 (1962/63)

FEWEST GOALS CONCEDED:
33 (1998/99)

MOST CLEAN SHEETS:
22 (1976/77)

FEWEST CLEAN SHEETS:
2 (1893/94)

FIRST TIME

FIRST LEAGUE GAME:
HOME v BOOTLE (03-SEP-1892)
RESULT: WON 7-0
FINAL POSITION: 5TH

MAN UTD

THEIR COMPLETE LEAGUE RECORD

P	W	D	L	F	A
3872	1764	952	1156	6579	5125

TOP SCORERS

SEASON	PLAYER	LGE GOALS
1999/2000	DWIGHT YORKE	20
1998/1999	DWIGHT YORKE	18
1997/1998	ANDY COLE	16
1996/1997	OLE SOLSKJAER	18
1995/1996	ERIC CANTONA	14

(All figures correct up to summer 2000)

KICKIN' OFF

SUCCESSIVE WINS AT START OF SEASON:
10 (1985/86)

SUCCESSIVE DEFEATS AT START OF SEASON:
12 (1930/31)

SUCCESSIVE UNBEATEN GAMES AT START OF SEASON:
15 (1985/86)

ON THE RUN

SUCCESSIVE GAMES UNBEATEN:
26 (04-FEB-1956)

SUCCESSIVE GAMES WITHOUT A WIN:
16 (03-NOV-1928), (19-APR-1930)

SUCCESSIVE WINS:
14 (15-OCT-1904)

SUCCESSIVE DEFEATS:
14 (26-APR-1930)

SUCCESSIVE DRAWS:
6 (30-OCT-1988)

SUCCESSIVE GAMES WITHOUT SCORING:
5 (22-FEB-1902), (26-JAN-1924), (07-FEB-1981)

SUCCESSIVE GAMES WITHOUT CONCEDING:
7 (15-OCT-1904), (20-SEP-1924)

HIGHS AND LOWS

BIGGEST HOME WIN:
10-1 v WOLVES (15-OCT-1892), 9-0 v WALSALL TS. (03-APR-1895), 9-0 v DARWEN (24-DEC-1898), 9-0 v IPSWICH (04 MAR-1995)

BIGGEST AWAY WIN:
7-0 v GRIMSBY TOWN (26-DEC-1899)

BIGGEST HOME DEFEAT:
0-6 v ASTON VILLA (14-MAR-1914) 1-7 v NEWCASTLE (10-SEP-1927), 0-6 v HUDDERSFIELD (10-SEP-1930)

BIGGEST AWAY DEFEAT:
0-7 v BLACKBURN (10-APR-1926), 0-7 v ASTON VILLA (27-DEC-1930), 0-7 v WOLVES (26-DEC-1931)

FIRST TIME

FIRST LEAGUE GAME:
AWAY v BLACKBURN ROVERS (03-SEP-1892)
RESULT: LOST 3-4
FINAL POSITION: 16TH

WIN, LOSE OR DRAW

MOST WINS (IN A SEASON):
28 (1905/06), (1956/57)

MOST DRAWS:
18 (1980/81)

MOST DEFEATS:
27 (1930/31)

GOALS

MOST GOALS SCORED (IN A SEASON):
103 (1956/57), (1958/59)

FEWEST GOALS SCORED:
38 (1901/02), (1973/74)

MOST GOALS CONCEDED:
115 (1930/31)

FEWEST GOALS CONCEDED:
23 (1924/25)

MOST CLEAN SHEETS:
25 (1924/25)

FEWEST CLEAN SHEETS:
2 (1893/94)

MIDDLESBROUGH

THEIR COMPLETE LEAGUE RECORD

P	W	D	L	F	A
3706	1413	899	1394	5632	5451

Boro had to settle for a mid-table position in the 1999-2000 season

TOP SCORERS

SEASON	PLAYER	LGE GOALS
1999/2000	HAMILTON RICARD	12
1998/1999	HAMILTON RICARD	15
1997/1998	MIKKEL BECK	14
1996/1997	FABRIZIO RAVANELLI	16
1995/1996	NICK BARMBY	7

(All figures correct up to summer 2000)

KICKIN' OFF

SUCCESSIVE WINS AT START OF SEASON:
4 (1925/26), (1993/94), (1994/95)

SUCCESSIVE DEFEATS AT START OF SEASON:
3 (1905/06), (1926/27), (1984/85), (1988/89)

SUCCESSIVE UNBEATEN GAMES AT START OF SEASON:
10 (1910/11)

WIN, LOSE OR DRAW

MOST WINS (IN A SEASON):
28 (1986/87)

MOST DRAWS:
19 (1924/25)

MOST DEFEATS:
27 (1923/24)

HIGHS AND LOWS

BIGGEST HOME WIN:
9-0 v BRIGHTON & HOVE A.
(23-AUG-1958)

BIGGEST AWAY WIN:
7-1 v BLACKBURN ROVERS
(29-NOV-1947), 7-1 v DERBY
COUNTY (29-AUG-1959)

BIGGEST HOME DEFEAT:
0-5 v BURY (12-FEB-1910) 0-5 v
HUDDERSFIELD TOWN
(25-AUG-1962) 1-6 v ARSENAL
(24-APR-1999)

BIGGEST AWAY DEFEAT:
0-9 v BLACKBURN ROVERS
(06-NOV-1954)

ON THE RUN

SUCCESSIVE GAMES UNBEATEN:
24 (08-SEP-1973)

SUCCESSIVE GAMES WITHOUT A WIN:
19 (03-OCT-1981)

SUCCESSIVE WINS:
9 (16-FEB-1974)

SUCCESSIVE DEFEATS:
8 (25-AUG-1954)

SUCCESSIVE DRAWS:
8 (03-APR-1971)

SUCCESSIVE GAMES WITHOUT SCORING:
4 (11 TIMES)

SUCCESSIVE GAMES WITHOUT CONCEDING:
7 (07-NOV-1987)

GOALS

MOST GOALS SCORED
(IN A SEASON): 122 (1926/27)

FEWEST GOALS SCORED:
34 (1981/82)

MOST GOALS CONCEDED:
91 (1953/54)

FEWEST GOALS CONCEDED:
30 (1973/74), (1986/87)

MOST CLEAN SHEETS:
27 (1986/87)

FEWEST CLEAN SHEETS:
4 (1927/28)

FIRST TIME

FIRST LEAGUE GAME:
AWAY v LINCOLN CITY
(02-SEP-1899)
RESULT: LOST 0-3
FINAL POSITION: 14TH

NEWCASTLE

THEIR COMPLETE LEAGUE RECORD

P	W	D	L	F	A
3864	1594	895	1375	6187	5529

TOP SCORERS

SEASON	PLAYER	LGE GOALS
1999/2000	ALAN SHEARER	23
1998/1999	ALAN SHEARER	14
1997/1998	JOHN BARNES	6
1996/1997	ALAN SHEARER	24
1995/1996	LES FERDINAND	25

(All figures correct up to summer 2000)

Steve Howey had an injury hit season at Newcastle last year

KICKIN' OFF

SUCCESSIVE WINS AT START OF SEASON:
11 (1992/93)

SUCCESSIVE DEFEATS AT START OF SEASON:
4 (1934/35)

SUCCESSIVE UNBEATEN GAMES AT START OF SEASON:
11 (1950/51), (1992/93), (1994/95)

ON THE RUN

SUCCESSIVE GAMES UNBEATEN:
14 (22-APR-1950)

SUCCESSIVE GAMES WITHOUT A WIN:
21 (14-JAN-1978)

SUCCESSIVE WINS:
13 (25-APR-1992)

SUCCESSIVE DEFEATS:
10 (23-AUG-1977)

SUCCESSIVE DRAWS:
4 (14 TIMES)

SUCCESSIVE GAMES WITHOUT SCORING:
6 (31-DEC-1938), (29-OCT-1988)

SUCCESSIVE GAMES WITHOUT CONCEDING:
6 (06-MAR-1982)

HIGHS AND LOWS

BIGGEST HOME WIN:
13-0 v NEWPORT COUNTY
(05-OCT-1946)

BIGGEST AWAY WIN:
6-0 v EVERTON (26-OCT-1912),
7-1 v MANCHESTER UTD
(10-SEP-1927), 6-0 v WALSALL
(29-SEP-1962)

BIGGEST HOME DEFEAT:
1-9 v SUNDERLAND
(05-DEC-1908)

BIGGEST AWAY DEFEAT:
0-9 v BURTON WANDERERS
(15-APR-1895)

FIRST TIME

FIRST LEAGUE GAME:
AWAY v WOOLWICH ARSENAL
(02-SEP-1893)
RESULT: DREW 2-2
FINAL POSITION: 4TH

WIN, LOSE OR DRAW

MOST WINS (IN A SEASON):
29 (1992/93)

MOST DRAWS:
17 (1990/91)

MOST DEFEATS:
26 (1977/78)

GOALS

MOST GOALS SCORED
(IN A SEASON):
98 (1951/52)

FEWEST GOALS SCORED:
30 (1980/81)

MOST GOALS CONCEDED:
109 (1960/61)

FEWEST GOALS CONCEDED:
35 (1969/70)

MOST CLEAN SHEETS:
20 (1947/48)

FEWEST CLEAN SHEETS:
3 (1933/34), (1960/61)

RANGERS

THEIR LEAGUE RECORD LAST SEASON

P	W	D	L	F	A
36	28	6	2	96	26

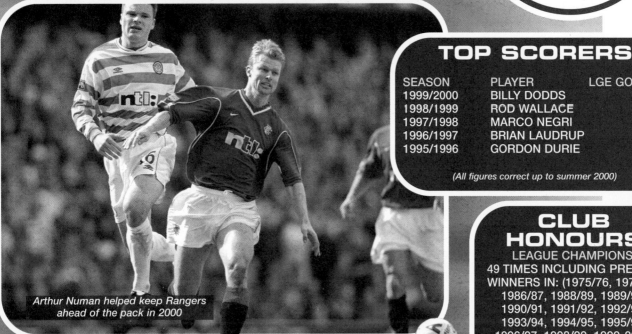

Arthur Numan helped keep Rangers ahead of the pack in 2000

TOP SCORERS

SEASON	PLAYER	LGE GOALS
1999/2000	BILLY DODDS	18
1998/1999	ROD WALLACE	17
1997/1998	MARCO NEGRI	32
1996/1997	BRIAN LAUDRUP	16
1995/1996	GORDON DURIE	17

(All figures correct up to summer 2000)

CLUB HONOURS

LEAGUE CHAMPIONS:
49 TIMES INCLUDING PREMIER WINNERS IN: (1975/76, 1977/78, 1986/87, 1988/89, 1989/90, 1990/91, 1991/92, 1992/93, 1993/94, 1994/95, 1995/96, 1996/97, 1998/99, 1999-2000)

SCOTTISH CUP WINNERS:
29 TIMES

SCOTTISH CUP RUNNERS-UP:
17 TIMES

SCOTTISH LEAGUE CUP WINNERS:
(1946/47, 1948/49, 1960/61, 1961/62, 1963/64, 1964/65, 1970/71, 1975/76, 1977/78, 1978/79, 1981/82, 1983/84, 1984/85, 1986/87, 1987/88, 1988/89, 1990/91, 1992/93, 1993/94, 1996/97, 1998/99)

SCOTTISH LEAGUE CUP RUNNERS-UP:
7 TIMES

EUROPEAN CUP WINNERS:
NONE

EUROPEAN CUP RUNNERS-UP:
NONE

EUROPEAN CUP-WINNERS' CUP WINNERS:
(1971/72)

EUROPEAN CUP-WINNERS' CUP RUNNERS-UP:
(1960/61, 1966/67)

UEFA CUP WINNERS/R-UP:
NONE

MOST CAPPED PLAYER

ALLY McCOIST 60 SCOTLAND

DEBUT v HOLLAND IN 1986, LAST APPEARANCE v ESTONIA IN 1999

HIGHS AND LOWS

MOST LEAGUE APPEARANCES:
JOHN GREIG (1962/1978) 496

RECORD ATTENDANCE:
118,567 V CELTIC
(2-JAN-1939)

BEST SCOTTISH LEAGUE TITLE WINNING SEQUENCE:
9 TIMES
(1988/89 TO 1996/97)

BIGGEST VICTORY:
14-2 v BLAIRGOWRIE
(20-JAN-1934)

BIGGEST DEFEAT:
2-10 v AIRDRIE
(1886)

RECORD BREAKERS

MOST LEAGUE GOALS SCORED BY A PLAYER (IN A SEASON):
SAM ENGLISH (1931/32) 44

MOST GOALS SCORED BY A PLAYER OVERALL:
ALLY McCOIST (1985/98) 355

BIGGEST FEE PAID OUT BY THE CLUB FOR A PLAYER
£5.5 MILLION FOR ANDREI KANCHELSKIS IN JULY 1998

BIGGEST FEE RECEIVED BY THE CLUB FOR A PLAYER:
£5.85 MILLION FROM MARSEILLE FOR TREVOR STEVEN IN AUG 1991

FIRST TIME

FIRST LEAGUE SEASON:
(1890/91)
FINAL POSITION: JOINT CHAMPIONS WITH DUMBARTON

SOUTHAMPTON

THEIR COMPLETE LEAGUE RECORD

P	W	D	L	F	A
3060	1159	784	1117	4627	4484

TOP SCORERS

SEASON	PLAYER	LGE GOALS
1999/2000	MARIAN PAHARS	13
1998/1999	EGIL OSTENSTAD	7
1997/1998	OSTENSTAD/LE TISSIER	11
1996/1997	MATT LE TISSIER	13
1995/1996	SHIPPERLEY/LE TISSIER	7

(All figures correct up to summer 2000)

KICKIN' OFF

SUCCESSIVE WINS AT START OF SEASON:
3 (1957/58), (1988/89)

SUCCESSIVE DEFEATS AT START OF SEASON:
5 (1998/99)

SUCCESSIVE UNBEATEN GAMES AT START OF SEASON:
7 (1950/51)

ON THE RUN

SUCCESSIVE GAMES UNBEATEN:
19 (05-SEP-1921)

SUCCESSIVE GAMES WITHOUT A WIN:
20 (30-AUG-1969)

SUCCESSIVE WINS:
6 (05-SEP-1964)

SUCCESSIVE DEFEATS:
5 (9 TIMES)

SUCCESSIVE DRAWS:
7 (28-DEC-1994)

SUCCESSIVE GAMES WITHOUT SCORING:
5 (26-AUG-1922), (01-SEP-1937)

SUCCESSIVE GAMES WITHOUT CONCEDING:
8 (17-APR-1922)

HIGHS AND LOWS

BIGGEST HOME WIN:
8-0 v NORTHAMPTON TOWN
(24-DEC-1921)

BIGGEST AWAY WIN:
6-0 v CARLISLE UTD
(22-JAN-1977)

BIGGEST HOME DEFEAT:
0-6 v PLYMOUTH ARGYLE
(05-DEC-1931),
0-6 v BRENTFORD (09-MAR-1959)

BIGGEST AWAY DEFEAT:
0-8 v TOTTENHAM HOTSPUR
(28-MAR-1936), 0-8 v EVERTON
(20-NOV-1971)

FIRST TIME

FIRST LEAGUE GAME:
AWAY v GILLINGHAM
(28-AUG-1920)
RESULT: DREW 1-1
FINAL POSITION: 2ND

WIN, LOSE OR DRAW

MOST WINS (IN A SEASON):
26 (1959/60)

MOST DRAWS:
18 (1924/25), (1972/73), (1994/95)

MOST DEFEATS:
23 (1971/72), (1993/94)

GOALS

MOST GOALS SCORED
(IN A SEASON):
112 (1957/58)

FEWEST GOALS SCORED:
37 (1998/99)

MOST GOALS CONCEDED:
92 (1966/67)

FEWEST GOALS CONCEDED:
21 (1921/22)

MOST CLEAN SHEETS:
26 (1921/22)

FEWEST CLEAN SHEETS:
3 (1952/53)

SUNDERLAND

THEIR COMPLETE LEAGUE RECORD

P	W	D	L	F	A
3982	1638	968	1376	6398	5722

Sunderland had plenty to celebrate last season

TOP SCORERS

SEASON	PLAYER	LGE GOALS
1999/2000	KEVIN PHILLIPS	30
1998/1999	KEVIN PHILLIPS	23
1997/1998	KEVIN PHILLIPS	29
1996/1997	RUSSELL/STEWART	4
1995/1996	CRAIG RUSSELL	13

(All figures correct up to summer 2000)

KICKIN' OFF

SUCCESSIVE WINS AT START OF SEASON:
4 (1894/95), (1903/04), (1910/11), (1925/26)

SUCCESSIVE DEFEATS AT START OF SEASON:
5 (1985/86)

SUCCESSIVE UNBEATEN GAMES AT START OF SEASON:
18 (1998/99)

WIN, LOSE OR DRAW

MOST WINS (IN A SEASON):
31 (1998/99)

MOST DRAWS:
18 (1954/55), (1994/95)

MOST DEFEATS: 22 (1956/57), (1969/70), (1984/85), (1992/93)

HIGHS AND LOWS

BIGGEST HOME WIN:
8-0 v DERBY COUNTY (01-SEP-1894)

BIGGEST AWAY WIN:
9-1 v NEWCASTLE UTD (05-DEC-1908)

BIGGEST HOME DEFEAT:
1-6 v NEWCASTLE UTD (26-DEC-1955), 1-6 v BIRMINGHAM CITY (05-APR-1958)

BIGGEST AWAY DEFEAT:
0-8 v THE WEDNESDAY (26-DEC-1911), 0-8 v WEST HAM UTD (19-OCT-1968), 0-8 v WATFORD (25-SEP-1982)

ON THE RUN

SUCCESSIVE GAMES UNBEATEN:
18 (10-FEB-1996) (08-AUG-1998)

SUCCESSIVE GAMES WITHOUT A WIN:
14 (16-APR-1985)

SUCCESSIVE WINS:
13 (14-NOV-1891)

SUCCESSIVE DEFEATS:
9 (23-NOV-1976)

SUCCESSIVE DRAWS:
6 (26-MAR-1949)

SUCCESSIVE GAMES WITHOUT SCORING:
10 (27-NOV-1976)

SUCCESSIVE GAMES WITHOUT CONCEDING:
6 (26-DEC-1901), (20-DEC-1902), (18-JAN-1964), (18-DEC-1982), (2-APR-1996)

GOALS

MOST GOALS SCORED (IN A SEASON):
109 (1935/36)

FEWEST GOALS SCORED:
30 (1969/70)

MOST GOALS CONCEDED:
97 (1957/58)

FEWEST GOALS CONCEDED:
28 (1998/99)

MOST CLEAN SHEETS:
26 (1995/96)

FEWEST CLEAN SHEETS:
3 (1952/53)

FIRST TIME

FIRST LEAGUE GAME:
HOME v BURNLEY (13-SEP-1890)
RESULT: LOST 2-3
FINAL POSITION: 7TH

TOTTENHAM

THEIR COMPLETE LEAGUE RECORD

P	W	D	L	F	A
3340	1384	825	1131	5487	4706

TOP SCORERS

SEASON	PLAYER	LGE GOALS
1999/2000	IVERSEN/ARMSTRONG	14
1998/1999	STEFFEN IVERSEN	9
1997/1998	JURGEN KLINSMANN	9
1996/1997	TEDDY SHERINGHAM	7
1995/1996	TEDDY SHERINGHAM	16

(All figures correct up to summer 2000)

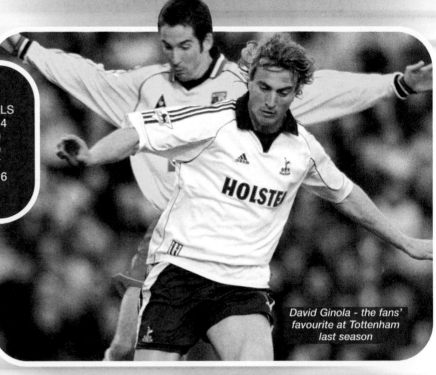

David Ginola - the fans' favourite at Tottenham last season

KICKIN' OFF

SUCCESSIVE WINS AT START OF SEASON:
11 (1960/61)

SUCCESSIVE DEFEATS AT START OF SEASON:
4 (1912/13), (1974/75)

SUCCESSIVE UNBEATEN GAMES AT START OF SEASON:
16 (1960/61)

HIGHS AND LOWS

BIGGEST HOME WIN:
9-0 v BRISTOL ROVERS (22-OCT-1977)

BIGGEST AWAY WIN:
5-0 v COVENTRY CITY (30-AUG-1919), 5-0 v PLYMOUTH ARGYLE (07-MAY-1949), 6-1 v STOKE CITY (15-SEP-1951), 6-1 v WEST HAM (25-AUG-1962), 5-0 v MILLWALL (29-APR-1989)

BIGGEST HOME DEFEAT:
0-6 v SUNDERLAND (19-DEC-1914), 0-6 v ARSENAL (06 MAR-1935)

BIGGEST AWAY DEFEAT: 0-7 v LIVERPOOL (02-SEP-1978)

WIN, LOSE OR DRAW

MOST WINS (IN A SEASON):
32 (1919/20)

MOST DRAWS: 17 (1968/69)

MOST DEFEATS:
22 (1934/35)

ON THE RUN

SUCCESSIVE GAMES UNBEATEN:
22 (31-AUG-1949)

SUCCESSIVE GAMES WITHOUT A WIN:
16 (29-DEC-1934)

SUCCESSIVE WINS:
13 (23-APR-1960)

SUCCESSIVE DEFEATS:
7 (01-JAN-1994)

SUCCESSIVE DRAWS:
5 (01-FEB-1969), (20-SEP-1975)

SUCCESSIVE GAMES WITHOUT SCORING:
6 (28-DEC-1985)

SUCCESSIVE GAMES WITHOUT CONCEDING:
5 (22-APR-1967), (24-JAN-1987), (17-DEC-1994)

FIRST TIME

FIRST LEAGUE GAME:
HOME v WOLVES (01-SEP-1908)
RESULT: WON 3-0
FINAL POSITION: 2ND

GOALS

MOST GOALS SCORED (IN A SEASON):
115 (1960/61)

FEWEST GOALS SCORED:
38 (1987/88)

MOST GOALS CONCEDED:
95 (1958/59)

FEWEST GOALS CONCEDED:
32 (1908/09), (1919/20)

MOST CLEAN SHEETS:
21 (1970/71)

FEWEST CLEAN SHEETS:
4 (1926/27)

WEST HAM

THEIR COMPLETE LEAGUE RECORD

P	W	D	L	F	A
3094	1183	760	1151	4714	4605

West Ham just failed to secure a place in the UEFA Cup

TOP SCORERS

SEASON	PLAYER	LGE GOALS
1999/2000	PAOLO DI CANIO	16
1998/1999	IAN WRIGHT	9
1997/1998	JOHN HARTSON	15
1996/1997	PAUL KITSON	8
1995/1996	TONY COTTEE	10

(All figures correct up to summer 2000)

KICKIN' OFF

SUCCESSIVE WINS AT START OF SEASON:
5 (1983/84)

SUCCESSIVE DEFEATS AT START OF SEASON:
3 (1938/39), (1962/63), (1966/67), (1971/72), (1977/78)

SUCCESSIVE UNBEATEN GAMES AT START OF SEASON:
21 (1990/91)

WIN, LOSE OR DRAW

MOST WINS (IN A SEASON):
28 (1980/81)

MOST DRAWS:
18 (1968/69)

MOST DEFEATS:
23 (1931/32)

HIGHS AND LOWS

BIGGEST HOME WIN:
8-0 v ROTHERHAM UNITED (08-MAR-1958), 8-0 v SUNDERLAND (19-OCT-1968)

BIGGEST AWAY WIN:
6-0 v LEICESTER CITY (15-FEB-1923)

BIGGEST HOME DEFEAT:
0-6 v SHEFFIELD WED (08-DEC-1951), 2-8 v BLACKBURN ROVERS (26-DEC-1963)

BIGGEST AWAY DEFEAT:
0-7 v BARNSLEY (01-SEP-1919), 0-7 v EVERTON (22 OCT-1927), 0-7 v SHEFFIELD WED (28-NOV-1959)

ON THE RUN

SUCCESSIVE GAMES UNBEATEN:
27 (27-DEC-1980)

SUCCESSIVE GAMES WITHOUT A WIN:
17 (31-JAN-1976)

SUCCESSIVE WINS:
9 (19-OCT-1985)

SUCCESSIVE DEFEATS:
9 (28-MAR-1932)

SUCCESSIVE DRAWS:
5 (07-SEP-1968)

SUCCESSIVE GAMES WITHOUT SCORING:
5 (01-MAY-1971)

SUCCESSIVE GAMES WITHOUT CONCEDING:
5 (11-NOV-1922), (29-SEP-1923), (18-APR-1981), (23-NOV-1985), (26-DEC-1990)

GOALS

MOST GOALS SCORED (IN A SEASON):
101 (1957/58)

FEWEST GOALS SCORED:
37 (1991/92)

MOST GOALS CONCEDED:
107 (1931/32)

FEWEST GOALS CONCEDED:
29 (1980/81)

MOST CLEAN SHEETS:
22 (1980/81)

FEWEST CLEAN SHEETS:
3 (1931/32)

FIRST TIME

FIRST LEAGUE GAME:
HOME v LINCOLN CITY (30-AUG-1919)
RESULT: DREW 1-1
FINAL POSITION: 7TH

THE BEST OF
LAST WORD
WHEN WAS THE LAST TIME YOU...

PAVEL SRNICEK
...SAW A GOOD FILM?
"One of the first things I did when I came to Britain was to install a satellite dish, so I could pick up Czech television. It was brilliant over Christmas as there were so many films on TV that reminded me of when I was a little boy back home."

FRANK LAMPARD
...SWAPPED SHIRTS?
"When we played Bournemouth in the Worthington Cup last season I gave my shirt to a lad called Claus Jorgensen. And when I took his in return he was really shocked that I actually wanted to take it."

JOE COLE
...PLAYED AN INSTRUMENT?
"I played the recorder at school but I was totally useless at it. All I was capable of producing were these hilarious, squeaky noises that got on my schoolmates' nerves."

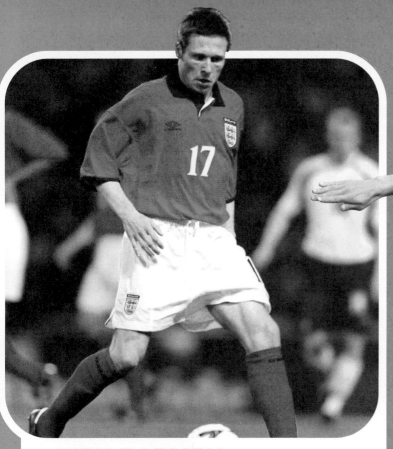

NICK BARMBY
...TOOK PART IN A QUIZ?
"We have quizzes on the coach when we go to away games, and quite often play Trivial Pursuit. I won't tell you who's the worst, but it must be true what they say about goalkeepers. Steve Simonsen and Paul Gerrard never seem to win."

JON HARLEY
...HAD A WEIRD DREAM?
"All the time - and they're always about football. I can remember one particular time when I was clean through on goal but my legs just wouldn't move. I just stood there."

KIERON DYER
...LET OFF A FIRE EXTINGUISHER?
"Hah! When I was at high school I used to be a bit of a rebel! I fired it at one of my mates. But I never got found out . It was a water type and not the foam - they're the best for really drenching someone!"

JOHN HARTSON
...FELT REALLY SCARED?
"Every time I go downstairs in the middle of the night to get a glass of water. I'm really afraid of the dark, which some people find hard to believe."

Shoot INTERACTIVE

DO YOU KNOW YOUR STARS OF THE FUTURE?

HOW MUCH HAVE YOU READ ABOUT THEM OVER THE LAST FEW PAGES? GET YOUR THINKING GEAR AROUND THIS AND WE'LL SEE...

1 Robbie Keane and Roy Keane are cousins. True or false?

2 What team did Joe Cole support when he was a kid? West Ham, Chelsea or Hamilton Academicals?

3 Who was Kieron Dyer's hero?

4 Against which country did Steven Gerrard make his full England debut last season?

5 From which club did Villa sign Gareth Barry?

6 Which of our young stars helped his country win the 1998 European Youth Championship?

LINK 'EM UP

CAN YOU JOIN THE CLUB NAMES AND GROUNDS TO THE CORRECT BADGES? WE'VE DONE THE FIRST ONE TO GET YOU GOING.

ASTON VILLA

CHARLTON

CHELSEA

EVERTON

MAN UTD

SUNDERLAND

OLD TRAFFORD

GOODISON PARK

VILLA PARK

STADIUM OF LIGHT

STAMFORD BRIDGE

THE VALLEY

WHAT'S GOIN' ON?

THE SNEAKY DESIGNER'S GONE AND MADE FIVE CHANGES TO PICTURE B, JUST TO TRY AND CATCH YOU OUT. CAN YOU SPOT 'EM?

Quiz answers on page 110-111

MARIAN PAHARS
SOUTHAMPTON

Shoot

Shoot

MARK KENNEDY
MAN CITY

EURO
STARS

RIVALDO
ZIDANE
McMANAMAN
BATISTUTA
VIERI

Also including...

Best of...Kit Bag

Shoot Interactive

Rivaldo is one of the most naturally talented footballers in the world and maintains the tradition that the Brazilians have for playing the beautiful game. The phrase 'he's got a sweet left foot' could have been invented for the silky midfielder, whose dribbling skills and range of passing are second to none. He also has an eye for goal, both from open play and set-pieces and, like so many of his countrymen, is lethal from free-kicks anywhere around goal.

The current World Player of the Year, he has few equals in the modern game.

WHO DOES HE PLAY FOR?

BARCELONA They have millions of fans around the world. The Catalan people who support the club in Spain are among the most fervent fans in the world and play a huge part in creating the atmosphere that makes Barcelona so special.

STADIUM: Nou Camp
CAPACITY: 112,000
STAR PLAYERS: Patrick Kluivert, Luis Figo, Frank de Boer
HOME STRIP: Blue and red halved shirts, blue shorts
HONOURS: Spanish title 1929, 1945, 1948, 1949, 1952, 1953, 1969, 1970,1974, 1985, 1991, 1992, 1993, 1994, 1998, 1999 (16 times); Spanish Cup 1910, 1912, 1913, 1920, 1922, 1925, 1926, 1928, 1942, 1951, 1952, 1953, 1957, 1959, 1963, 1968, 1971, 1978, 1981, 1983, 1988,1990, 1997, 1998 (24 times); European Cup 1992; European Cup-Winners' Cup 1979, 1982, 1989, 1997; UEFA Cup 1977, 1990, 1993; Fairs Cup (UEFA Cup) 1958, 1960, 1966; European Super Cup 1992, 1998

DID YOU KNOW?

The first team Rivaldo played for was his local side, Santa Cruz. As he had no money, he sometimes had to walk up to 25 kilometres (16 miles) to training. No wonder he's fit!

His son, Rivaldinho - which means 'Little Rivaldo' - has starred in several adverts for Coca-Cola.

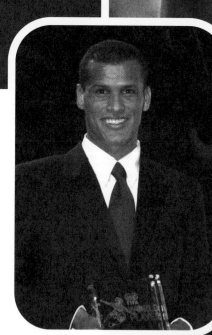

He sends his children to an English-speaking school in Barcelona because he never had the chance to learn languages as a child.

One of Rivaldo's most treasured memories is winning the Copa America Final against Uruguay in 1999. Brazil won 3-0 and he scored twice in the game.

FACT FILE
NAME   Rivaldo Victor Borba Ferreira
BORN   April 19, 1972 in Recife, Brazil
HONOURS   Spanish title 1998, 1999;
Spanish Cup 1998; Super Cup 1998;
Brazilian title 1994; Sao Paolo State
Championship 1996; European
Footballer of the Year 1999, World
Footballer of the Year 1999
PREVIOUS CLUBS   Santa Cruz,
Mogi-Mirim, Corinthians, Palmeiras (all
Brazil), Deportivo La Coruna (Spain)
INTERNATIONAL HONOURS   Brazil full
caps; World Cup runner-up 1998; Copa
America 1999; Olympic bronze 1996

YOU WHAT?

SPANISH FOOTBALL IS AMONG THE TOUGHEST IN THE WORLD, RIVALDO. IS THERE A LOT OF PRESSURE PLAYING FOR BARCELONA?

"I experienced greater pressure playing in Brazil, for Corinthians and Palmeiras, than at Barcelona. The pressure in Brazil is a little menacing. If you lose the game the fans make threats and they can be violent."

HOW EXCITED WERE YOU TO BE NAMED THE WORLD'S BEST PLAYER?

"To be named World Footballer of the Year is something I was very proud of. Now I have to carry on what I'm doing and maintain the will to play my best ability all of the time."

YOU HAVE BEEN LINKED WITH MAN UNITED IN THE PAST. WOULD YOU LIKE TO PLAY IN ENGLAND?

"One day I might play in England. At the moment I'm happy at Barcelona but you never know what might happen in the future. I would like to return to Brazil at some stage in my career. If I could choose anywhere I would go back to Palmeiras."

HOW LONG DO YOU THINK YOU CAN PLAY AT THE TOP?

"I will try to play for as many years as I can. But when the fans start whistling at you, that's the moment to stop."

YOU WERE CRITICISED AT HOME A LOT WEREN'T YOU?

"When I was younger I wasn't valued by the press in Brazil. The fans valued me, but not the press. Now they rate me as well!"

RIVALDO
Barcelona & Brazil

ZINEDINE ZIDANE
Juventus & France

Zinedine Zidane is the complete midfield player. The French maestro has everything - strength, vision, superb passing ability and an eye for goal, as he proved to stunning effect in the 1998 World Cup Final when he netted twice for his country as they beat Brazil 3-0. That match secured his place among the superstars of world football.

WHO DOES HE PLAY FOR?

JUVENTUS The name is known throughout the world and wherever you travel you will always find youngsters wearing the Italian club's famous black and white striped shirts. The tradition of the legendary club is such that they are feared throughout European football and when people talk about the best teams in the world, Juve are never far from the top of the list.

STADIUM: Delle Alpi
CAPACITY: 69,041
STAR PLAYERS: Alessandro Del Piero, Edgar Davids, Filippo Inzaghi
HOME STRIP: Black and white striped shirts, black shorts
HONOURS: Italian League title 1905, 1926, 1931, 1932, 1933, 1934,1935, 1950, 1952, 1958, 1960, 1961, 1967, 1972, 1973, 1975, 1977, 1978,1981, 1982, 1984, 1986, 1995, 1997, 1998 (25 times); Italian Cup 1938, 1942, 1959, 1960, 1965, 1979, 1983, 1990, 1995 (nine times); European Cup 1985, 1996; European Cup-Winners' Cup 1984; UEFA Cup 1977, 1990, 1993; European Super Cup 1984, 1997; World Club Cup 1985, 1996

DID YOU KNOW?

Zinedine Zidane is a bit of a mouthful for his team-mates, so he is known as ZZ or Zizou.

When he is not playing, Zidane's hobbies include painting, basketball, music and going to the cinema.

He named his first son Enzo, after his boyhood idol Enzo Francescoli, who was a star player with Marseille, Torino and Uruguay. One of his most prized possessions is a shirt given to him by Francescoli.

His ambition was to play for his home-town club, Marseille but he has yet to achieve that. He began his career with Cannes and also played for Bordeaux.

FACT FILE

NAME: Zinedine Zidane
BORN: June 23, 1972 in Marseille, France
HONOURS: Italian title: 1997, 1998; European Super Cup 1997; European Footballer of the Year 1998; FIFA World Player of the Year 1998; 1998 World Cup winner; Euro 2000 winner
PREVIOUS CLUBS: Cannes, Bordeaux
INTERNATIONAL HONOURS: France Youth, U21, full caps; World Cup 1998

YOU WHAT?

LAST SEASON'S ITALIAN TITLE WAS A CLOSE RUN THING, ZINEDINE. IT MUST HAVE BEEN DISAPPOINTING TO LOSE OUT TO LAZIO IN THE END?
"Yes, losing the Serie A title on the last day was my biggest disappointment in football. It was even worse than losing two successive European Cup Finals."

Juventus have got many fine players, but you have been described as the best. How do you feel about that?
"One player alone cannot make a team win. I know that I am important to the Juventus side, but for that very reason it's vital that I prove this again and again."

You were voted the 'World Player of the Year' in 1998. That must have been a great honour for you?
"I've never really considered myself the world's greatest player, but I would do anything to achieve that status."

Is it difficult for you, as a Frenchman, playing all of your football in Italy?
"When I first arrived in Turin it was difficult for me to communicate, yes. I couldn't find the right words. Now it's different and I can make myself heard - which is good!"

Who has been the biggest influence on your career?
"Marcello Lippi, who was in charge at Juventus for a few years, has been the most important coach of my career. He gave me the will to win. I don't know how, but he managed to communicate to me extremely positive things. I will always be thankful to him for that."

FACT FILE
NAME: Steve McManaman
BORN: February 11, 1972 in Liverpool
HONOURS: FA Cup 1992; League Cup 1995, European Cup 2000
PREVIOUS CLUBS: Liverpool
INTERNATIONAL HONOURS England Youth, U21 and full caps

STEVE McMANAMAN
Real Madrid & England

On his day, Steve McManaman is one the most difficult players for any defender to play against. With his loping running style and quick feet he has the ability to play on either wing and can go past his marker with ease. If there is a criticism of him it is that he does not score enough goals and is not consistent enough, but you don't play for Liverpool and Real Madrid unless you are quality - and he is!

YOU WHAT?

HOW ARE YOU ENJOYING LIVING IN SPAIN THEN, STEVE?
"Madrid is a fantastic city and I like the lifestyle. The pace of life is so relaxed and I seem to fit in really easily. I haven't felt homesick at all."

WHAT ABOUT ON THE PITCH. WHAT'S THE STYLE OF PLAY LIKE?
"There isn't much difference between playing in Spain and for Liverpool. All the top teams are technically very good and every game is a big one when you play for a great club like Real or Liverpool."

IT MUST HAVE BEEN A TOUGH DECISION TO LEAVE LIVERPOOL?
"I was extremely sad to leave Liverpool, but the opportunity to play for Real Madrid was too good to turn down. It allowed me to achieve my ambition to test myself in another top European league."

WHAT HAVE YOU FOUND DIFFICULT ABOUT PLAYING IN SPAIN?
"One of the strangest things for me to get used to in Spain was playing on Sundays and having such late kick-offs. It took a while to adjust to after being used to playing at three o'clock on a Saturday afternoon."

REAL MADRID ARE ONE OF THE BIGGEST CLUBS IN THE WORLD. THAT MUST BRING ITS OWN PRESSURES?
"The fans here expect us to win and they let us know about it when they think we have let them down. Madrid must attack at all costs and sometimes it costs us."

WHO DOES HE PLAY FOR?

REAL MADRID One of the great names of European football, Real Madrid are famous the world over with their distinctive all-white strip. They were the first truly brilliant side, dominating the European Cup in its early years and winning the first five competitions. Their bitter rivalry with Barcelona is one of the fiercest anywhere in the game, but Real hold the upper-hand at the moment after winning the European Cup for a record eighth time last May following their thrilling 3-0 victory over fellow countrymen Valencia in Paris.

STADIUM: Santiago Bernabeu
CAPACITY: 106,500
STAR PLAYERS: Raul, Fernando Redondo, Roberto Carlos
HOME STRIP: All white
HONOURS: Spanish League title 1932, 1933, 1954, 1955, 1957, 1958, 1961, 1962, 1963, 1964, 1965, 1967, 1968, 1969, 1972, 1975, 1976, 1978, 1979, 1980, 1986, 1987, 1988, 1989, 1990, 1995, 1997 (27 times); Spanish Cup 1905, 1906, 1907, 1908, 1917, 1934, 1936, 1946, 1947, 1962, 1970, 1974, 1975, 1980, 1982, 1989, 1993 (17 times); European Cup 1956, 1957, 1958, 1959, 1960, 1966, 1998, 2000 (eight times); UEFA Cup 1985, 1986; World Club Cup 1960, 1998

DID YOU KNOW?

Known as Shaggy by his team-mates, Steve has been recognisable in recent years by his long flowing locks. It's a far cry from the old days, when he used to have his hair cut by his mum!

His favourite food is garlic prawns, and he likes to wash them down with a pint of his favourite beer, Guinness.

He is big mates with his former Liverpool and England pal Robbie Fowler having grown up with him at Anfield. He and Robbie part-own a racehorse called 'Another Horse'.

Steve's disciplinary record is excellent, but if he is ever called up to defend himself in front of the FA he could have a bit of a head start. His girlfriend, Victoria Edwards, is a qualified barrister!

Steve has always been a good runner. He was a schoolboy athletics star and once beat the Great Britain Olympic athlete Curtis Robb in a schools' cross-country race.

FACT FILE
NAME: Gabriel Batistuta
BORN: February 1, 1969 in
Reconquista, Argentina
HONOURS: Italian Cup 1996
PREVIOUS CLUBS: Santa Fe,
Newell's Old Boys, River Plate,
Boca Juniors (all Argentina),
Fiorentina (Italy)
INTERNATIONAL HONOURS
Argentina full caps; Copa
America winner 1991

GABRIEL BATISTUTA
Roma & Argentina

Batistuta is a legend of the modern game and one of the most feared strikers of his generation.

His pace and strength make him a danger to any defence - although he is equally effective with his back to goal - while his unerring ability to hit the target with either foot from all angles and distances means he has all the attributes to succeed at the top level, as his goals record in Italy proves. It's not for nothing that his adoring fans in Italy and Argentina refer to him as 'Batigol'.

DID YOU KNOW?

The player he most admired as a boy was striker Mario Kempes, who helped Argentina win the World Cup in 1978.

In 1997, he was dropped from the Argentine national team under coach Daniel Passarella - coz he refused to cut his long hair!

His hobbies away from football are hunting and fishing. He also enjoys playing tennis.

His favourites film is 'As Good As It Gets', starring Jack Nicholson. His favourite musicians are old rockers Bruce Springsteen and Phil Collins.

He never watches himself, or any football on TV for that matter.

He was so popular at his previous club Fiorentina that supporters erected a life-size bronze statue of him outside the ground. When he joined Roma, many of the club's fans cried in the streets.

WHO DOES HE PLAY FOR?

ROMA They have been in the shadow of their local rivals Lazio for a few years now, but will be hoping Batistuta can lead them to their first Serie A title since 1983.

STADIUM: Olympic Stadium, Rome
CAPACITY: 83,000
STAR PLAYERS: Francesco Totti, Vincenzo Montella, Marco Delvecchio
HOME STRIP: Claret shirt, white shorts, claret socks
HONOURS: Italian League title 1942, 1983; Italian Cup 1964, 1969, 1980, 1981, 1984, 1986, 1991; European Fairs Cup (UEFA Cup) 1961

YOU WHAT?

DOES IT BOTHER YOU, GABRIEL, THAT YOU HAVEN'T WON MANY TROPHIES IN YOUR CAREER?
"I hope I don't look back on my career without winning a major tournament with either my club or my country. I love the game, but football is about success and that has been in short supply in my career."

WHAT'S BETTER, ITALIAN FOOTBALL OR THE ENGLISH GAME?
"The football in Italy is still the best and the best players in the world want to come here. You have to be at the top of your game to make it here."

THERE WAS A LOT OF FUSS WHEN YOUR NATIONAL COACH ASKED YOU TO CUT YOUR HAIR AND YOU REFUSED, WASN'T THERE?
"I don't think anyone has the right to tell me what I should look like. My wife doesn't complain, and she's the only one I would cut my hair for."

DO YOU FANCY EVER COMING TO PLAY IN ENGLAND?
"I would really like to play one or two years in English football some time. I have that idea very much in my head and I hope it will happen. Manchester United is where I would like to go. But I think perhaps it is too late now."

YOU ARE A HERO TO MANY PEOPLE. DOES THAT MAKE YOU HAPPY?
"I always try to set a good example. I can't do more than that. It would make me very happy if one parent came up to me and said: 'My son is growing up in this way because he is attempting to imitate you'."

IT MUST HAVE BEEN TOUGH TO LEAVE THE FIORENTINA FANS?
"Yes, the fans there were great to me but the time felt right for a new challenge and to take the next stage in my career."

CHRISTIAN VIERI
Inter Milan & Italy

Vieri became the most expensive player in the world when he joined Inter from Lazio in 1999 for an amazing £27 million and is now one of the most feared strikers in the game. His strength, finishing ability and aerial power make him a hero of the Italian fans and the number one striker in his country.

WHO DOES HE PLAY FOR?

INTER MILAN Milan is one of the great cities of world football, boasting two of Europe's most famous and glamorous teams - AC and Internazionale. With their distinctive strip of blue and black striped shirts, Inter are recognised everywhere and dominated Italian and European football in the 1960s. But incredibly they have not won the Italian Championship since 1989 and have fallen behind their local rivals AC in terms of trophies. However, with the likes of Vieri and a fully fit Ronaldo, surely they will end their sorry run soon as they look to rule the city of Milan once more.

STADIUM: Giuseppe Meazza (San Siro)
CAPACITY: 85,443
STAR PLAYERS: Ronaldo, Javier Zanetti, Ivan Zamorano
HOME STRIP: Blue and black striped shirts, black shorts
HONOURS: Italian title 1910, 1920, 1930, 1938, 1940, 1953, 1954, 1963, 1965, 1966, 1971, 1980, 1989 (13 times); Italian Cup 1939, 1978, 1982; European Cup 1964, 1965; UEFA Cup 1991, 1994, 1998; World Club Cup 1964, 1965

DID YOU KNOW?

Christian's nickname is Bobo, a reference to his father, Roberto, who was often called Bob.

His favourite athlete is the American basketball star Dennis Rodman.

His favourite actor is Sylvester Stallone, and his favourite actress is the star of Notting Hill and Erin Brokovich, Julia Roberts.

He scored Italy's 1000th international goal against Moldova in a World Cup qualifier in March 1997. It was his senior debut, so he made quite an impression.

His boyhood idol was not a footballer, but the Australian cricket captain Allan Border. He grew up in Sydney after his family moved there from Italy when he was three, and he still speaks English with an Australian accent.

FACT FILE

NAME: Christian Vieri
BORN: July 12, 1973 in Bologna, Italy
HONOURS: Italian title 1996; European Cup-Winners' Cup 1999
PREVIOUS CLUBS: Prato, Torino, Pisa, Ravenna, Venezia, Atalanta, Juventus, Atletico Madrid, Lazio
INTERNATIONAL HONOURS: Italian U21, full caps

YOU WERE BORN IN ITALY, CHRISTIAN, BUT GREW UP IN AUSTRALIA. WAS IT TOUGH TO GO BACK TO ITALY WHEN YOU KICKED OFF YOUR CAREER?
"It wasn't easy to leave my parents as a child. When I was 14 I moved to Italy but I used to cry every day. I wanted to go back home. My dad took me home and I was going to stay in Australia for ever. But after two weeks I felt the need for Italy again. I used to say to myself 'if you want to be a footballer you cannot stay here'."

YOU CREATED QUITE A FUSS EARLIER IN YOUR CAREER, WHEN YOU SEEMED TO CHANGE CLUBS EVERY YEAR...
"Take a record book and check players' careers: a lot of them have travelled as much as me. The thing is, now people only talk about me. Anyway, when you change you get better."

BUT WHY DID YOU NEED TO MOVE?
"It seems I had to keep moving to keep developing my game. It was difficult, changing teams so often, but on the other hand I also learned a lot from the experience of working at different clubs, learning from different coaches and team-mates."

YOU ARE NOW REGARDED AS ONE OF THE WORLD'S BEST STRIKERS. THAT MUST MEAN A LOT OF PRESSURE?
"I've been under pressure for so long, I don't notice. Moving to Juve helped, that was when it hit me that I wanted to be a winner - and accepting everything that went with it."

THE BEST OF
KIT BAG

JULIAN JOACHIM
Who's the maddest player at Villa?
"David James is totally off his head and is completely crazy. He can talk for fun and goes on and on if you're not careful! Some might say Ugo Ehiogu, though, because of his dress sense! I won't reveal what he wears but Ugo does have a few outfits which have the lads in stitches."

ANDY JOHNSON **IF YOU COULD CHANGE ONE THING ABOUT THE GAME WHAT WOULD IT BE?**
"The referees - I just wouldn't have any! They need changing and I would let them use their own knowledge a bit more."

DARREN EADIE **TELL US A FUNNY FOOTBALL STORY.**
"Our physio told Chris Sutton to tape an aspirin to his ankle, saying that the sweat would dissolve it and he'd feel better. He actually did it!"

ALAN KIMBLE HAVE YOU EVER DELIBERATELY KICKED AN OPPONENT? "Of course I have, and I don't know of any player that hasn't clipped heels during their career - they just don't admit it! I'm too slow these days!"

LEE SHARPE WHAT'S BEEN YOUR MOST EMBARRASSING MOMENT? "That was when I scored my first goal for Man U - a right footer from just inside the box. I ran towards the Stretford End and went to slide on my knees. But my knee got stuck in the ground and I went head first into the turf - right in front of all the fans!"

CEDRIC ROUSSEL HOW DID YOU FIRST GET INTO FOOTBALL? "When I was about four years-old. I was crying because I was afraid, but my dad pushed me onto the pitch. After five minutes I found that I loved it."

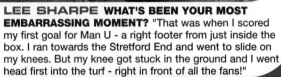

STEVE GUPPY WHAT'S THE WEIRDEST THING THAT HAS EVER HAPPENED TO YOU? "I got followed home by this girl. After about 10 minutes I realised she was following me and this went on for about an hour. I pulled over and bought her an ice lolly and she seemed to be alright after that. Weird!"

SHAUN NEWTON IF YOU HAD A HOT DATE THE NIGHT BEFORE A GAME, WOULD YOU GO? "No. I like to spend plenty of time before a match thinking about the game ahead. I've already got a girlfriend, anyway!"

Shoot INTERACTIVE

DO YOU KNOW YOUR EURO STARS?
SO, YOU RECKON YOU'VE GOT IT ALL SUSSED OUT EH? BEST GET ANSWERING THESE QUIRKY QUESTIONS THEN...

1 What trophy did Rivaldo win with Brazil in 1999?

2 Name one of Zinedine Zidane's previous clubs.

3 Steve McManaman won which club competition with Real Madrid last season?

4 By what name was Gabriel Batistuta known by the Fiorentina fans?

5 In which country did Christian Vieri grow up? Was it Italy, Australia or Croatia?

6 Which of our Euro Stars once played for a side called Mogi-Mirim?

TRIPLE CHANCE
Look at the questions below, and then check out the answers. Only one of them is right, of course, but which one? Ring the one you think is correct and check out if you're right, at the end!

1 Where do West Ham play all their home games?
A. Hammers Stadium
B. Hillsborough
C. Upton Park

2 For what country has Everton's Don Hutchison won international caps?
A. England
B. Scotland
C. Trinidad & Tobago

3 Which pop star is David Beckham married to?
A. Posh Spice
B. Louise
C. Natalie Appleton

4 Of which Premiership club is Joe Royle manager?
A. Southampton
B. Man City
C. Everton

5 Which England international top scored in the Premiership last season?
A. Kevin Phillips
B. Alan Shearer
C. Robbie Fowler

WARP FACTOR

Ooops! Looks like things went all weird on us when we slipped through that Black Hole back there. Can you help the crew of the good ship Shoot to work out who these nine wobbly footballers arc?

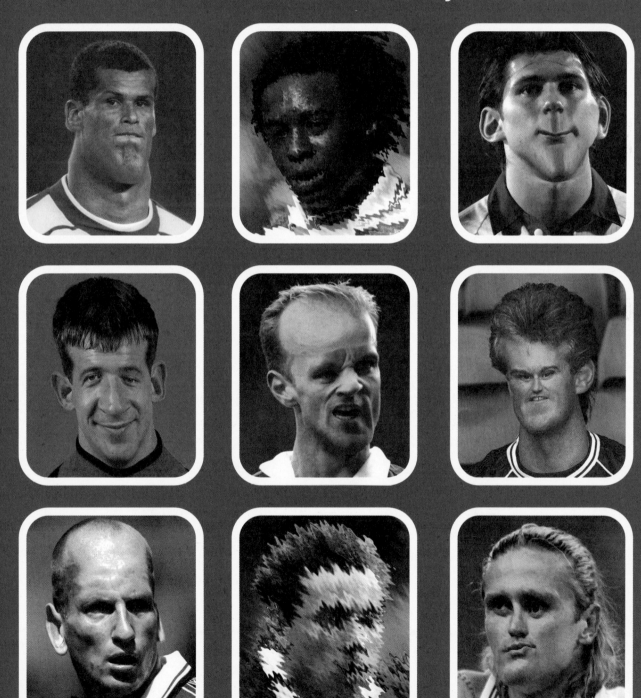

Quiz answers on page 110-111

CHELSEA

LEICESTER CITY

Shoot

MARK KINSELLA
CHARLTON ATHLETIC

Shoot

ANDY O'BRIEN
BRADFORD CITY

Shoot

BERKOVIC BECKHAM GINOLA DI CANIO KEWELL BER
DI CANIO KEWELL BERKOVIC BECKHAM GINOLA

KEWELL BERKOVIC BECKHAM GINOLA DI CANIO KEWELL BERKOVIC BECKHAM GINOLA

THE
ENTERTAINERS

DI CANIO
KEWELL
BERKOVIC
BECKHAM
GINOLA

Also including...

Euro 2000...England's agony

Shoot Interactive

PAOLO DI CANIO
WEST HAM

DI CANIO ON...

...HEADING BACK TO ITALY TO FINISH HIS CAREER

"I'm getting on a bit now, so it's very unlikely that I'll be heading back to Italy to play before I retire. I enjoyed some brilliant times in Serie A and played with some wonderful players - you are facing world class stars every week. You can't beat playing for the likes of Juventus, Milan, Lazio or Napoli."

...PLAYING FOR THE HAPPY HAMMERS

"Things can always change, of course, but I'm very happy at West Ham at the moment. I've never experienced an atmosphere like at this club. It is also special for me to have a manager like Harry Redknapp, who believes in me."

...ENGLISH SUPPORTERS

"It's always good to build a relationship with the fans. The Celtic and Sheffield Wednesday supporters were brilliant to me and now the West Ham crowd have taken to me as well. I always give 100 per cent commitment when I play and my attitude is always to be positive. It is an honour to play for a club like West Ham, so I try to play my best in every game. The fans pay good money to follow us and it's our duty to perform for them."

...PUSHING REFS OVER

"Like a lot of Italians I used to swing my arms about when I was unhappy. I know I am not the same now and I can keep my temper a lot better. I run more and speak to myself more as I am playing, instead of getting so angry with things. It has taken some time, but in Italy we say the same as you do in English: 'Better late than never'."

...FOLLOWING VINNIE JONES INTO ACTING

"Vinnie was brilliant in 'Lock, Stock and Two Smoking Barrels' - the role was perfect for him. It is

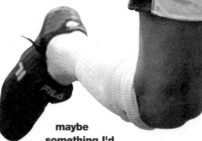

maybe something I'd consider being involved in when I stop playing - I once appeared in a short film for a young directors' festival in Rome. But for now I want to concentrate on my football and helping West Ham do well in the Premiership."

HERE'S A LOOK AT SOME OF PAOLO'S GREATEST MOMENTS...

DATELINE: Upton Park, March 20, 1999
MATCH: West Ham 2 Newcastle 0
MAGIC MOMENT: di Canio scores his second Hammers' goal with a fantastic individual effort. Picking up a ball from Paul Kitson outside the area he glides through the Newcastle defence before rounding goalkeeper Shay Given to stroke the ball into the net. Pure class!

DATELINE: Upton Park, March 26, 2000
MATCH: West Ham 2 Wimbledon 1
MAGIC MOMENT: A inch-perfect long cross from Trevor Sinclair in the eighth minute drops over the head of Wimbledon defender Kenny Cunningham and into the path of the on-rushing di Canio. The Italian leaves the ground, twists in the air and volleys the ball with the outside of his right foot, sending it screaming past Neil Sullivan and into the net. They can stop the voting for 'Goal of the Season' straight away. What a finish!

ANOTHER HAMMERS LEGEND
TONY COTTEE

Still going strong at Leicester City, pint-sized striker Tony Cottee began his career with the Hammers nearly twenty years ago. He scored 118 goals for them before moving to Everton for a then huge fee of £2.3m in August 1988. He returned to Upton Park in September 1994, playing another 76 games, before moving, via Malaysia, to Leicester. With seven England caps to his credit, he won his first major trophy last season - the Worthington Cup - with the Filbert Street club.

HARRY KEWELL
LEEDS & AUSTRALIA

KEWELL ON...

....CHOOSING TO PLAY FOR AUSTRALIA AHEAD OF ENGLAND
"Australia is where I was born, so I don't know why people thought I'd choose to play for England! I'm proud of my country and I'm honoured to play for them. I know that football is behind sports like cricket and rugby back home, but it's catching up fast."

...PLAYING AGAINST GALATASARAY LAST YEAR
"It was an intimidating atmosphere out there and was a very sad occasion as well. In the home match, I was sent-off but I never touched their player and couldn't believe it when the ref showed me the red card."

...FOREIGNERS IN THE PREMIERSHIP
"There are more and more players being drawn to the Premier because it's exciting, it's quick and there are loads of goals. It's the best League in the world at the moment - as simple as that. Everybody wants to be a part of it, and you can't blame them."

...HIS STYLE OF PLAY
"I've always thought that the only way to achieve something in life is to go out and get it - and that's the same with football. Once I get the ball I just go for it, and if anyone gets in my way I do my best to go round them. If it works, great, if it doesn't then I'm confident enough to think that it will the next time."

...CHILLING OUT
"It can be quite hard to unwind, but I do like playing a bit of golf. Me and Lee Bowyer are the best at the club when we play together... we can take anyone! On our own we're pretty average, but when we get together we just seem to click and both play really well. It's a great way of relaxing."

...WINNING AWARDS
"Obviously being named PFA Young Player of the Year last season was a special moment for me. Being saluted by your fellow pros is very satisfying."

ANOTHER LEEDS LEGEND
GORDON STRACHAN
The current Coventry boss was an inspired signing by Leeds boss Howard Wilkinson in March 1989. A battling and skilful midfielder, Strachan seemed to be coming towards the end of his career when he left Man Utd for Elland Road. But instead he inspired Leeds to promotion from the old Second Division in 1990, followed by the League title just two years later. A Scottish international, he tasted European glory early in his career, winning the Cup-Winners' Cup with Aberdeen in 1983.

HERE'S A LOOK AT SOME OF HARRY'S GREATEST MOMENTS.

DATELINE: Elland Road, March 5, 2000
MATCH: Leeds 3 Coventry 0
MAGIC MOMENT: Kewell is both maker and taker as Leeds stay hot on the heels of Man Utd. He drives in an unstoppable shot from an Ian Harte free kick after just five minutes, and shortly before half-time his perfect pass sets Michael Bridges free for United's second.

DATELINE: Elland Road, September 18, 1999
MATCH: Leeds 2 Middlesbro' 0
MAGIC MOMENT: Receiving a loose ball 25 yards out, Kewell looks up and calmly smashes it past 'keeper Mark Schwarzer.

DATELINE: Elland Road, March 9, 2000
MATCH: Leeds 1 AS Roma 0
MAGIC MOMENT: A magnificent goal midway through the second-half earns Leeds a place in the UEFA Cup Quarter-Final. Good work from Eirik Bakke and Lee Bowyer creates a half-chance for Kewell, who makes space for himself before unleashing a swerving, dipping shot from way outside the area that flies into the net.

EYAL BERKOVIC
CELTIC & ISRAEL

BERKOVIC ON...

...HIS FIRST YEAR AT CELTIC
"It was disappointing and rather difficult. I'm not saying that I didn't enjoy it - I did - but we didn't achieve what I, or the club, expected. There were far too many problems on and off the field for Celtic to deal with. We keep looking forward though."

...THE OLD FIRM GAMES
"They are impossible to explain if you haven't experienced them! I've played in London 'derbies' for West Ham and they have been frantic, but the old firm games are totally different. The atmosphere is incredible and you can hardly think. But although I love playing on these occasions, it's difficult to enjoy them. It can be like war on the field, and that does not make for very good football!"

...MOVING BACK TO ENGLAND ONE DAY
"One day I would like to return to England and that's where I hope to finish my career. But football is a strange game and you can never be sure of anything. I still have three years left on my contract at Celtic and I definitely want to see them out."

...WINNING THE LEAGUE TITLE
"I didn't come to Parkhead to be second best. What would be the point of that? Celtic are not just a big club - they are a massive club. We should never have to settle for second best and this season want to lead us to the title."

...MOVING TO MAN UTD
"Every player dreams of turning out for a club like United. They are the biggest club in the world at the moment and I'm sure there's not a player out there who would think differently. But we can't all play for them and I'm very lucky to be playing for a huge club like Celtic."

ANOTHER CELTIC LEGEND
HENRIK LARSSON

Having missed a huge chunk of last season with a badly broken leg, recovering just in time for Euro 2000, Henrik Larsson was looking forward to the 2000/2001 campaign to get his club career back on track. Having joined the club in the summer of 1997, Larsson has already earned himself legend status at Parkhead, scoring the goals which earned Celtic a long-overdue League title in 1997/98, stopping Rangers winning a record ten Championships in a row in the process. The Swedish international netted 29 in 35 games the following year to underline his worth to the side.

3
FANTASTIC ACHIEVEMENTS

HERE'S A LOOK AT SOME OF EYAL'S GREATEST MOMENTS.

DATELINE: White Hart Lane, April 24, 1999
MATCH: Tottenham 1 West Ham 2
MAGIC MOMENT: Playing against a Spurs side that have recently tried to buy him, Eyal Berkovic shows just what they've been missing. A brilliant playmaking display is capped by two killer passes to set up West Ham's goals for Ian Wright and Marc Keller.

DATELINE: The Dell, October 26, 1996
MATCH: Southampton 6 Man Utd 3
MAGIC MOMENT: Eyal turns in a majestic performance as the double-winners are humbled at The Dell. Neat backheels and fancy flicks keep the crowd on their feet throughout and Saints are already 4-2 up when Berkovic scores his second of the afternoon, a powerful shot after a corner is half-cleared.

DATELINE: Parkhead, April 2, 2000
MATCH: Celtic 4 Kilmarnock 2
MAGIC MOMENT: The Israeli star is stretchered off with a rib injury towards the end of the game - but not before he has almost single-handedly won the points for Celtic. He's already had one effort disallowed when he receives a pass from Johan Mjallby on 73 minutes and lifts the ball over the advancing Gordon Marshall to put Celtic 3-2 up. It's a great way to celebrate his 28th birthday.

DAVID BECKHAM
Man Utd & England

BECKHAM ON...

...HIS FAMOUS TEMPER
"It's just that I'm a passionate player, and it can be hard sometimes not to react to all of the insults and provocation I receive. Eric Cantona found himself in the same situation as me, but I've learned to accept it now. I'm a far from vicious or violent person. I would never look to deliberatey hurt or injure an opponent."

...NOT DOING MANY INTERVIEWS. EXCEPT WITH SHOOT, OF COURSE
"It's a sad situation, but it got to the point where journalists were trying to trap me and make me say things I didn't want to say. They were more interested in my private life than my football, which is a shame because I love talking about football."

...LEAVING MAN UTD
"I've never even considered leaving Old Trafford. But after the 1998 World Cup people were wondering how it would go for me staying in this country - whether I'd be able to cope with the pressure. All I wanted to do was get home and get playing again. Playing for United is very important to me, I've supported them all my life."

...HIS CROSSING SKILLS
"Actually, most of our attacking moves come from down the left, but I do get involved sometimes and I enjoy it when I do. Any time I can get to the byline and put a decent cross in I feel like I'm really making a contribution to the team. When you have players of the quality of Dwight Yorke and Andy Cole up front all you have to do is pop the ball on their heads - it's my job to do that."

...ALEX FERGUSON
"Sir Alex has brought me up and made my career since I joined United. We all owe the manager everything. I was so pleased when he was knighted. When someone like him gets honoured you have to say it's well deserved. He's so totally consistent and he's always there for the United lads."

ANOTHER RED DEVILS LEGEND
ERIC CANTONA

Back in the days when there were only a handful of foreign stars in the Premiership, Eric Cantona was comfortably the best of the bunch. A brilliant attacking midfielder with superb control and a gift for the unexpected, he turned United from nearly-men to the country's most powerful side. He inspired the Old Trafford club to four League titles but, true to form, when he'd had enough he simply walked away - from United and from football - in May 1997.

3
FANTASTIC
ACHIEVEMENTS

HERE'S A LOOK AT SOME OF DAVID'S GREATEST MOMENTS.

DATELINE: Selhurst Park, August 17, 1996

MATCH: Wimbledon 0 Man Utd 3
MAGIC MOMENT: The goal that made David Beckham famous. It's the last minute of the opening game of 1996-97 when Becks receives the ball five yards inside his own half. He looks up, spots Dons' keeper Neil Sullivan off his line and sends the ball sailing over his head and into the net - from fully 55 yards! It's the undisputed goal of the season, almost before the campaign has kicked-off.

DATELINE: Lens, France, June 26, 1998

MATCH: Colombia 0 England 2
MAGIC MOMENT: Half-an-hour in to this crucial World Cup group game and England are already a goal up as they are awarded a free-kick just outside the Colombia penalty area. Up steps David Beckham to curl the ball over the wall for his first international goal.

DATELINE: Old Trafford, April 19, 2000

MATCH: Man Utd 2 Real Madrid 3
MAGIC MOMENT: With United 3-0 down to the Spanish giants, David Beckham steps up to score one of the best goals of his career. Picking the ball up on the edge of the Madrid area he drifts past three defenders before rifling the ball into the corner of the net.

DAVID GINOLA
SPURS & FRANCE

GINOLA ON...

...THE ENGLISH SUPPORTERS

"They are brilliant - just amazing. The fans in England are the best in the world, there's no doubt about it. They have passion and live, breathe and sleep football. As a player I am very proud to play in England, there is no other place where you can enjoy the game so much."

...STAYING IN ENGLAND WHEN HIS CAREER IS OVER

"Why not? It would not be a big deal as I have a son and daughter who both speak good English and who go to school here. But one day I would like to go back to France and go fishing and do other simple things."

...PLAYING FOR GEORGE GRAHAM AT SPURS

"I'm quite an experienced player now, so I think the manager will have more of an effect on the younger lads in the squad. For me it is a little bit different, but I've learned from every manager I've played with. I believe George Graham is definitely the right man for Spurs."

...LOVING HIS FOOTBALL

"It's always a good day when I step onto a football pitch. That means I'm fit to play and football can be so exciting. I realised from a young age I had a special talent and I've always loved this game. I'm lucky to have the chance to play this game every week and you get some moments that are so special on the football pitch."

...HIS CHARITY WORK

"I'm in a position where people will listen to things I say and they'll believe that what people like myself say is right. So it is important to put across the right message - footballers are role models. I'm lucky to be in such a privileged position. But I want to use the power I have to be helpful."

ANOTHER SPURS LEGEND
TEDDY SHERINGHAM

A treble winner with Man Utd the season before last, and a League Champion again in 1999-2000, 'Super Ted' spent five happy years at White Hart Lane after signing from Nottingham Forest for £2.1m in August 1992. A star for England at Euro 96, Teddy won 38 caps for his country, as well as scoring 99 goals in 200 games for Spurs. Strength in the air and the ability to pick out team-mates with a telling pass or flick make him a valuable front-man.

FANTASTIC ACHIEVEMENTS

HERE'S A LOOK AT SOME OF DAVID'S GREATEST MOMENTS.

DATELINE: St. James' Park, October 29, 1996
MATCH: Newcastle 4 Ferencvaros 0
MAGIC MOMENT: An outstanding Ginola goal caps a great team performance in this UEFA Cup Second Round tie. The Frenchman sells an outrageous dummy on his left foot before flicking the ball over the wrong-footed defence back onto his right and rifling home an unstoppable volley. Pure class.

DATELINE: Selhurst Park, January 23, 1999
MATCH: Wimbledon 1 Spurs 1
MAGIC MOMENT: Having been accused by opponents Wimbledon of being a 'diver', Ginola strikes back in style in this FA Cup Fourth Round match. Seventy-two minutes in, his pace and power takes him past three Dons defenders before hitting a powerful low shot past Neil Sullivan.

DATELINE: Oakwell, March 16, 1999
MATCH: Barnsley 0 Tottenham 1
MAGIC MOMENT: Ginola settles this FA Cup Quarter-Final with a goal of stunning brilliance. An hour of the game has passed before the skilful winger picks the ball up near the left touchline. He weaves past four defenders before sliding the ball under the advancing Tony Bullock to score one of the great individual goals of the season.

AGONY... ECSTASY... & AGONY AGAIN

England's mixed memories of Euro 2000

David Seaman celebrates England's 1-0 win over Germany....

Phil Neville's lunge gives Romania a last minute penalty, they scored and England went out of Euro 2000

*Paul Scholes gives England a dream start
against Portugal - but it ended in a 3-2 defeat*

...thanks to this headed goal from England skipper Alan Shearer

Shoot INTERACTIVE

DO YOU KNOW YOUR ENTERTAINERS?

HOPEFULLY YOU WERE WELL ENTERTAINED IN THAT LAST CHAPTER - BUT HOW MUCH NOTICE WERE YOU TAKING? TACKLE THESE AND FIND OUT...

1 Paolo di Canio won the Italian League with Inter Milan. True or false?

2 For which country does Harry Kewell play international football?

3 Name two of the British clubs that Eyal Berkovic has played for.

4 To who does David Beckham reckon he owes everything? Is it (a) his son, Brooklyn, (b) his mum and dad, or (c) Sir Alex Ferguson?

5 Which fans does David Ginola think are the best in the world?

6 Which of our entertainers has not won full caps for his country?

QUICK FIRE ROUND

GIVE YOURSELF 60 SECONDS - OR A MINUTE IF YOU LIKE - AND SEE HOW MANY OF THE FOLLOWING QUESTIONS YOU CAN GET RIGHT.

1 Alan Curbishley is the manager of which Premiership club?

2 Name the side that play their home matches at Valley Parade.

3 Does Ryan Giggs play on the left-wing or the right-wing?

4 From which club did Kevin Phillips join Sunderland?

5 Which Premiership side does James Scowcroft play for?

6 Nigel Martyn plays in goal for which team?

7 Which club are nicknamed The Toffees?

8 Who was voted as Player of the Year in England last season?

9 If Larsson scored past Klos, which two sides would be in action?

10 Derby's Mart Poom plays in which position?

COLOUR 'EM IN

OUR NASTY DESIGNERS HAVE TAKEN THE COLOUR OUT OF THIS PICTURE OF
MIDDLESBROUGH'S BRIAN DEANE AND LIVERPOOL'S SAMI HYYPIA. SHOW US YOUR
COLOURING SKILLS BY BRIGHTENING UP THE PICTURE WITH YOUR OWN
WICKED LOOK FOR TWO NEW FOOTBALL KITS.

Quiz answers on page 110-111

Shoot

MUZZY IZZET
LEICESTER CITY

IPSWICH TOWN

FIRST DIVISION PLAY-OFF WINNERS

Shoot

SHOOT INTERACTIVE ANSWERS

FROM PAGE 30-31

Do you know your Super Strikers?
1. Nigeria. 2. True. 3. Chris Waddle. 4. Defence. 5. Croatia Zagreb. 6. It took Arsenal to the Cup-Winners' Cup Final.

Who are ya?
1. Kieron Dyer 2. David Ginola

Wordsearch

FROM PAGE 70-71

Do you know your Stars of the Future?
1. False. 2. Chelsea. 3. John Barnes. 4. Ukraine. 5. Brighton. 6. Robbie Keane (Ireland).

Link 'em up

Aston Villa	Villa Park
Charlton	The Valley
Chelsea	Stamford Bridge
Everton	Goodison Park
Man Utd	Old Trafford
Sunderland	Stadium of Light

What's goin' on?
1. Di Matteo now has a yellow sock; Carbone's hand is missing; Leboeuf now has a wrist band; player in background now has yellow hair; the ball has moved around.

FROM PAGE 88-89

Do you know your Euro Stars?
1. The Copa America. 2. Cannes and Bordeaux. 3. Champions League. 4. Batigol. 5. Australia. 6. Rivaldo

Triple Chance
1. C - Upton Park. 2. B - Scotland. 3. A - Posh Spice. 4. B - Man City. 5. A - Kevin Phillips

Warp Factor!
Reading across top from left to right: Rivaldo, Reggie Blinker, Frank Lampard, Nigel Martyn, Dennis Bergkamp, Didier Deschamps, Jaap Stam, Andrei Kanchelskis, Emmanuel Petit.

FROM PAGE 106-107

Do you know your Entertainers?
1. False - he won it with AC Milan. 2. Australia. 3. Southampton, West Ham and Celtic. 4. C - Sir Alex Ferguson. 5. English fans (of course!). 6.Paolo di Canio.

Quickfire Round
1.Charlton 2. Bradford. 3. Left-wing. 4. Watford. 5. Ipswich. 6. Leeds. 7. Everton. 8. Roy Keane. 9. Celtic v Rangers. 10. Goalkeeper.